Wisdom in the University

This provocative and challenging book questions how people think about what universities should seek to do and how they should respond to the grave problems of our age. It addresses issues such as:

- What is wisdom?
- Ought universities to seek, promote and teach wisdom and what would this involve?
- Does it mean we need a revolution in the aims and methods of academic inquiry?
- What implications would the pursuit of wisdom have for science, for social inquiry and the humanities, for education?
- Is it reasonable to ask of universities that they take up the task of helping humanity learn how to create a wiser world?
- Is there a religious dimension to wisdom?
- What can non-academics do to encourage universities to take wisdom seriously?
- Would the pursuit of wisdom be possible given that universities are increasingly subjected to commercial pressures?

With contributions from leading experts in various fields, *Wisdom in the University* is essential reading for all those interested in the future of universities and philosophy of education.

This book was previously published as a special issue of *London Review of Education*.

Ronald Barnett is Pro-Director for Longer Term Strategy and Professor of Higher Education at the Institute of Education, University of London.

Nicholas Maxwell is Emeritus Reader in Philosophy of Science and Honorary Senior Research Fellow at University College London.

Wisdom in the University

Edited by Ronald Barnett and Nicholas Maxwell

Routledge
Taylor & Francis Group

LONDON AND NEW YORK

First published 2008 by Routledge
2 Park Square, Milton Park, Abingdon, Oxon, OX14 4RN

Simultaneously published in the USA and Canada
by Routledge
270 Madison Ave, New York NY 10016

Routledge is an imprint of the Taylor & Francis Group, an informa business

Transferred to Digital Printing 2009

© 2008 Taylor & Francis

Typeset in Gills Sans by Genesis Typesetting Ltd, Rochester, Kent

British Library Cataloguing in Publication Data
A catalogue record for this book is available from the British Library

ISBN10: 0-415-44934-0 (hbk)
ISBN10: 0-415-49557-1 (pbk)

ISBN13: 978-0-415-44934-2 (hbk)
ISBN13: 978-0-415-49557-8 (pbk)

CONTENTS

Wisdom in the university

We live in troubled times. There are the conflicts in Iraq and in Afghanistan and their questionable elements of imperialism, the violence in areas such as Darfur and Chechnya, and the continuing Israeli/Palestinian conflict. There is the threat of international terrorism, and the responses to terrorism by the US, UK and other democratic nations. There is the enduring poverty of millions in Africa and other parts of the developing world; and the poverty in some of the advanced countries is actually worsening. There is the arms trade, and the spread of modern armaments, conventional, chemical, biological, and nuclear. There is the destruction of tropical rain forests and other natural habitats, and the rapid extinction of species on land and in the sea. And over everything hangs global warming, which is already beginning to unleash droughts, storms, floods and rising sea levels, all of which may cause populations to try to migrate, leading in turn, no doubt, to further conflict and war.

In the light of these threats and prospects, humanity urgently needs to learn how to manage its affairs somewhat more wisely than it has done so far. If any existing institutions are to take a lead in this matter, it must surely be our universities, the most advanced institutions of learning that we possess. But do universities devote themselves to helping humanity learn how to create a better world? Do they even conceive of their task, their rationale, in such terms?

Somewhere, lurking in the background, inherited from the past, there is, perhaps, the idea that universities should seek and promote wisdom. But this is hardly what, in reality, the modern university is about. Officially, the intellectual aim of inquiry is to acquire knowledge, and develop technological know-how. In addition, it is the job of universities to train students for the professions: the law, medicine, engineering, education, and so on. And increasingly, these days, a vitally necessary ancillary task for universities is to acquire funds. Once upon a time, the standing of a scientist or scholar in his or her university would depend on the quality of research. Now, increasingly, it seems to depend on the amount of funds brought into the university. Helping humanity learn how to create a better world is hardly at the forefront of academic concern.

Why not? How ought universities to be organized if they are to help humanity acquire a bit more wisdom? What ought to be the aims and methods, the structure and character, of academic inquiry if it is to be devoted rationally to helping us learn how to resolve our conflicts and social problems in more peaceful, just and cooperative ways than we do at present? What needs to change if universities are to teach and promote wisdom, as a deliberate policy rather paying wisdom lip service at the most? How can universities best serve the best interests of humanity?

These are the questions the papers of this special issue of the *London Review of Education* try to answer.

Maxwell argues, boldly and starkly, that we need a revolution. The basic official aim of inquiry at present is to acquire knowledge. But this, Maxwell argues, betrays both reason and humanity. If universities are to help humanity learn how to create a better world, in a rigorous and effective way, a revolution is needed in the whole organization and character of academic inquiry so that problems of living are put at the heart of the enterprise, and the basic aim becomes that of promoting wisdom—wisdom being understood to be the capacity to realize what is of value in life, for oneself and others, thus including knowledge and technological know-how, but much else besides.

Iredale considers to what extent Maxwell's call for revolution, from knowledge to wisdom, has been answered since it was first made some 30 years ago. He concludes that there has been some movement towards wisdom-inquiry independently of Maxwell's neglected call for it. The scientific community is today far more actively concerned with environmental problems and the social impact of science than it was three decades ago.

McHenry discusses the manner in which commercial pressures have adversely affected scientific research. He considers specific examples of drug companies distorting or repressing empirical findings of drug trials. It is not just that the priorities of research are adversely affected; the objectivity and independence of medical science has, in some cases, been undermined.

Sternberg *et al.* and Trowbridge are concerned with the question of how education can be conducted so that it leads to the acquisition of wisdom. Sternberg *et al.* discuss teaching for wisdom in schools. They spell out how education can be conducted in such a way that wisdom can be acquired along with whatever else is being taught and learned. Trowbridge gives an account of educational courses for older and retired people, designed specifically to enable these students to acquire wisdom.

Taking her lead from Aquinas and Newman, Deane-Drummond discusses ways in which theological perspectives on wisdom can bring enrichment to universities. She emphasizes the value of interdisciplinarity, community life, and ways of knowing other than the scientific, stressing that theologically informed wisdom could counteract the pathologies of religious extremism, creationism and intelligent design. She concludes by considering two issues of public concern: environmental issues, and new reproductive technologies.

Finally Nordstrom, in an essay that might be regarded as an object lesson in how to conduct teaching for wisdom, sets out to discover what can be learned about wisdom from Shakespeare. For Nordstrom, Shakespeare reveals to us what wisdom is by depicting countless varieties of its opposite: folly. However, we are not necessarily bound to be foolish. From time to time, in Shakespeare's plays, 'sparks of wisdom shine out against the general gloom of human inanity and insanity'.

Nicholas Maxwell
Ronald Barnett

From knowledge to wisdom: the need for an academic revolution

Nicholas Maxwell

Introduction

> Things fall apart; the centre cannot hold;
> Mere anarchy is loosed upon the world,
> The blood-dimmed tide is loosed, and everywhere
> The ceremony of innocence is drowned;
> The best lack all conviction, while the worst
> Are full of passionate intensity.
> (William Butler Yeats, 1950, p. 211. Reprinted by permission of A P Watt Ltd on behalf of
> Gráinne Yeats, Executrix of the Estate of Michael Butler Yeats)

The world today is beset with problems. Most serious of all, perhaps, there is the impending problem of global warming. There is the problem of the progressive destruction of tropical rainforests and other natural habitats, with its concomitant devastating extinction of species. There is the problem of war, over 100 million people having died in countless wars in the twentieth century (which compares unfavourably with the 12 million or so killed in wars during the nineteenth century). There is the arms trade, the massive stockpiling of armaments, even by poor countries, and the ever-present threat of their use by terrorists or in war, whether the arms be conventional, chemical, biological or nuclear.

There is the sustained and profound injustice of immense differences of wealth across the globe, the industrially advanced first world of North America, Europe and elsewhere experiencing unprecedented wealth while hundreds of millions of people live in conditions of poverty in the developing world, hungry, unemployed, without proper housing, healthcare, education, or even access to safe water. There is the long-standing problem of the rapid growth of the world's population, especially pronounced in the poorest parts of the world, and adversely affecting efforts at development. And there is the AIDS epidemic, again far more terrible in the poorest parts of the world, devastating millions of lives, destroying families, and crippling economies.

And, in addition to these global crises, there are problems of a more diffuse, intangible character, signs of a general cultural or spiritual malaise. There is the phenomenon of political apathy: the problems of humanity seem so immense, so remorseless, so utterly beyond human control, and each one of us, a mere individual, seems wholly impotent before the juggernaut of history. The new global economy can seem like a monster out of control, with human beings having to adapt their lives to its demands, rather than gaining support from it. There is the phenomenon of the trivialization of culture, as a result, perhaps, of technological innovation such as TV and the Internet. Once, people created and participated in their own live music, theatre, art, poetry. Now this is pumped into our homes and into our ears by our technology, a mass-produced culture for mass consumption; we have become passive consumers, and the product becomes ever more trivial in content. And finally, there is the phenomenon of the rise of religious and political fanaticism and terrorism opposed, it can seem, either in a faint-hearted and self-doubting way, or brutally by war and the suspension of justice, apparently confirming Yeats's lines 'The best lack all conviction, while the worst are full of passionate intensity'.

From knowledge to wisdom

What can be done in response to global problems such as these? There are a multitude of things that can be done, and *are* being done, in varying degrees, with varying amounts of success. Here, I wish to concentrate on just *one* thing that could be done, which would go to the heart of the above global problems, and to the heart of our apparent current incapacity to respond adequately to these problems.

We need to bring about a wholesale, structural revolution in the aims and methods, the entire intellectual and institutional character of academic inquiry. At present academic inquiry is devoted to acquiring *knowledge*. The idea is to acquire knowledge, and then apply it to help solve social problems. This needs to change, so that the basic aim becomes to seek and promote *wisdom*— wisdom being understood to be the capacity to realize what is of value in life for oneself and others (and thus including knowledge, know-how and understanding). Instead of devoting itself primarily to solving problems of knowledge, academic inquiry needs to give intellectual priority to the task of discovering possible solutions to problems of living.

The social sciences need to become social philosophy, or social methodology, devoted to promoting more cooperatively rational solving of conflicts and problems of living in the world. Social inquiry, so pursued, would be intellectually more fundamental than natural science. The natural sciences need to recognize three domains of discussion: evidence, theories, and aims. Problems concerning research aims need to be discussed by both scientists and non-scientists alike, involving as they do questions concerning social priorities and values. Philosophy needs to become the sustained rational exploration of our most fundamental problems of understanding; it also needs to take up the task of discovering how we may improve our personal, institutional and global aims and methods in life, so that what is of value in life may be realized more successfully. Education needs to change so that problems of living become more fundamental than problems of knowledge, the basic aim of education being to learn how to acquire wisdom in life. Academic inquiry as a whole needs to become somewhat like a people's civil service, having just sufficient power to retain its independence and integrity, doing for people, openly, what civil services are supposed to do, in secret, for Governments. These and many other changes, affecting every branch and aspect of academic inquiry, all result from replacing the aim to acquire knowledge by the aim to promote wisdom by cooperatively rational means (see Maxwell, 1976, 1984, 2004).

The crisis of science without wisdom

It may seem surprising that I should suggest that changing the aims and methods of academic inquiry would help us tackle the above global problems. It is, however, of decisive importance to appreciate that *all* the above global problems have arisen because of a massive increase in scientific knowledge and technology without a concomitant increase in global wisdom. Degradation of the environment due to industrialization and modern agriculture, global warming, the horrific number of people killed in war, the arms trade and the stockpiling of modern armaments, the immense differences in the wealth of populations across the globe, rapid population growth: all these have been made possible by the rapid growth of science and technology since the birth of modern science in the seventeenth century. Modern science and technology are even implicated in the rapid spread of AIDS in the last few decades. It is possible that, in Africa, AIDS has been spread in part by contaminated needles used in inoculation programmes; and globally, AIDS has spread so rapidly because of travel made possible by modern technology. And the more intangible global problems indicated above may also have come about, in part, as a result of the rapid growth of modern science and technology.

That the rapid growth of scientific knowledge and technological know-how should have these kinds of consequence is all but inevitable. Scientific and technological progress massively increases our power to act: in the absence of wisdom, this will have beneficial consequences, but will also have harmful ones, whether intended, as in war, or unforeseen and unintended (initially at least), as in environmental degradation. As long as we lacked modern science, lack of wisdom did not matter too much: our power to wreak havoc on the planet and each other was limited. Now that our power to act has been so massively enhanced by modern science and technology, global wisdom has become, not a luxury, but a necessity.

The crisis of our times, in short—the crisis behind all the others—is the crisis of science without wisdom. Having a kind of academic inquiry that is, by and large, restricted to acquiring knowledge can only serve to *intensify* this crisis. Changing the nature of science, and of academic inquiry more generally, is the key intellectual and institutional change that we need to make in order to come to grips with our global problems—above all, the global problem behind all the others, the crisis of ever-increasing technological power in the absence of wisdom. We urgently need a new kind of academic inquiry that gives intellectual priority to promoting the growth of global wisdom.

The damaging irrationality of knowledge-inquiry

There are those who simply blame scientific rationality for our problems. Scientific rationality needs to be restrained, it is argued, by intuition and tradition, by morality or religion, by socialism, or by insights acquired from the arts or humanities: (see Marcuse, 1964; Laing, 1965; Roszak, 1973; Feyerabend, 1978, 1987; Berman, 1981; Schwartz, 1987; Appleyard, 1992). But this kind of response profoundly misses the point. What we are suffering from is not too much reason, but not enough. Scientific rationality, so-called, is actually a species of damaging *irrationality* masquerading as rationality. Academic inquiry as it mostly exists at present, devoted to the growth of knowledge and technological know-how— *knowledge-inquiry* I shall call it (Maxwell, 1984, chapters 2 and 6)—is actually profoundly irrational when judged from the standpoint of contributing to human welfare. Judged from this all-important standpoint, knowledge-inquiry violates three of the four most elementary, uncontroversial rules of reason that one can conceive of (to be indicated in a moment). And that knowledge-inquiry is grossly irrational in this way has everything to do with its tendency to generate the kind of global problems considered above. Instead of false simulacra of reason, what we so urgently need is authentic reason devoted to the growth of wisdom.

Knowledge-inquiry demands that a sharp split be made between the social or humanitarian aims of inquiry and the *intellectual* aim. The intellectual aim is to acquire knowledge of truth, nothing being presupposed about the truth. Only those considerations may enter into the intellectual domain of inquiry relevant to the determination of truth— claims to knowledge, results of observation and experiment, arguments designed to establish truth or falsity. Feelings and desires, values, ideals, political and religious views, expressions of hopes and fears, cries of pain, articulation of problems of living: all these must be ruthlessly excluded from the intellectual domain of inquiry as having no relevance to the pursuit of knowledge—although of course inquiry can seek to develop factual knowledge about these things, within psychology, sociology or anthropology. Within natural science, an even more severe censorship system operates: an idea, in order to enter into the intellectual domain of science, must be an empirically testable claim to factual knowledge.

The basic idea of knowledge-inquiry, then, is this. First, knowledge is to be acquired; then it can be applied to help solve social problems. For this to work, authentic objective knowledge must be acquired. Almost paradoxically, human values and aspirations must be excluded from the intellectual domain of inquiry so that genuine factual knowledge is acquired and inquiry can be of genuine human value, and can be capable of helping us realize our human aspirations.[1]

This is the conception of inquiry which, I claim, violates reason in a wholesale, structural and damaging manner.

But what do I mean by 'reason'? As I use the term here, rationality appeals to the idea that there are general methods, rules or strategies which, if put into practice, give us our best chance, other things being equal, of solving our problems, realizing our aims. Rationality is an aid to success, but does not guarantee success, and does not determine what needs to be done.

Four elementary rules of reason, alluded to above, are:

1. Articulate and seek to improve the specification of the basic problem(s) to be solved.
2. Propose and critically assess alternative possible solutions.
3. When necessary, break up the basic problem to be solved into a number of *specialized* problems—preliminary, simpler, analogous, subordinate problems—(to be tackled in accordance with Rules 1 and 2), in an attempt to work gradually toward a solution to the basic problem to be solved.
4. Inter-connect attempts to solve the basic problem and specialized problems, so that basic problem-solving may guide, and be guided by, specialized problem-solving.

No enterprise which persistently violates (1) to (4) can be judged rational. If academic inquiry is to contribute to the aim of promoting human welfare, the quality of human life, by intellectual means, in a rational way, in a way that gives the best chances of success, then (1) to (4) must be built into the whole institutional/intellectual structure of academic inquiry.

In order to see that current academic inquiry, devoted primarily to the pursuit of knowledge, does indeed violate three of the above four rules of reason (when viewed from the standpoint of contributing to human welfare), two preliminary points need to be noted about the nature of the *problems* that academic inquiry ought to be trying to help solve.

First, granted that academic inquiry has, as its fundamental aim, to help promote human welfare by intellectual and educational means,[2] then the *problems* that inquiry fundamentally ought to try to help solve are problems of living, problems of action. From the standpoint of achieving what is of value in life, it is what we *do*, or refrain from doing, that ultimately matters. Even where new knowledge and technological know-how are relevant to the achievement of what is of value—as it is in medicine or agriculture, for example—it is always what this new knowledge or technological know-how enables us to *do* that matters. All the global problems discussed above require, for their resolution, not merely new knowledge, but rather new policies, new institutions, new ways of living. Scientific knowledge, and associated technological know-how have, if anything, as we have seen, contributed to the creation of these problems in the first place. Thus problems of living—problems of poverty, ill-health, injustice, deprivation—are solved by what we do, or refrain from doing; they are not solved by the mere provision of some item of knowledge (except when a problem of living *is* a problem of knowledge).

Second, in order to achieve what is of value in life more successfully than we do at present, we need to discover how to resolve conflicts and problems of living in more *cooperatively rational* ways than we do at present. There is a spectrum of ways in which conflicts can be resolved, from murder or all out war at the violent end of the spectrum, via enslavement, threat of murder or war, threats of a less extreme kind, manipulation, bargaining, voting, to cooperative rationality at the other end of the spectrum, those involved seeking, by rational means, to arrive at that course of action which does the best justice to the interests of all those involved. A basic task for a kind of academic inquiry that seeks to help promote human welfare must be to discover how conflict resolution can be moved away from the violent end of the spectrum towards the cooperatively rational end.

Granted all this, and granted that the above four rules of reason are put into practice then, at the most fundamental level, academic inquiry needs to:

1. Articulate, and seek to improve the articulation of, personal, social and global problems of living that need to be solved if the quality of human life is to be enhanced (including those indicated above).
2. Propose and critically assess alternative possible solutions—alternative possible *actions, policies, political programmes, legislative proposals, ideologies, philosophies of life.*

In addition, of course, academic inquiry must:

3. Break up the basic problems of living into subordinate, specialized problems—in particular, specialized problems of knowledge and technology.
4. Inter-connect basic and specialized problem-solving.

Academic inquiry as it mostly exists at present can be regarded as putting (3) into practice to splendid effect. The intricate maze of specialized disciplines devoted to improving knowledge and technological know-how that go to make up current academic inquiry is the result. But, disastrously, what we have at present, academic inquiry devoted primarily to improving knowledge, fails to put (1), (2) and (4) into practice. In pursuing knowledge, academic inquiry may articulate problems of knowledge, and propose and critically assess possible solutions, possible claims to knowledge—factual theses, observational and experimental results, theories. But, as we have seen, problems of *knowledge* are not (in general) problems of *living*; and solutions to problems of *knowledge* are not (in general) solutions to problems of *living*. Insofar as academia does at present put (1) and (2) into practice, in departments of social science and policy studies, it does so only at the periphery, and not as its central, fundamental intellectual task.

In short, academic inquiry devoted primarily to the pursuit of knowledge, when construed as having the basic humanitarian aim of helping to enhance the quality of human life by intellectual means, fails to put the two most elementary rules of reason into practice (Rules 1 and 2). Academic inquiry fails to do (at a fundamental level) what it most needs to do, namely (1) articulate problems of living, and (2) propose and critically assess possible solutions. And furthermore, as a result of failing to explore the basic problems that need to be solved, academic inquiry cannot put the fourth rule of rational problem-solving into practice either, namely (4) interconnect basic and specialized problem-solving. As I have remarked, *three* of the four most elementary rules of rational problem-solving are violated. (For a more detailed development of this argument see Maxwell, 1980, 1984, 2004.)

This gross structural irrationality of contemporary academic inquiry, of knowledge-inquiry, is no mere formal matter. It has profoundly damaging consequences for humanity. As I have pointed out above, granted that our aim is to contribute to human welfare by intellectual means, the basic problems we need to discover how to solve are problems of living, problems of action, not problems of knowledge. In failing to give intellectual priority to problems of living, knowledge-inquiry fails to tackle what most needs to be tackled in order to contribute to human welfare. In devoting itself to acquiring knowledge in a way that is unrelated to sustained concern about what humanity's most urgent problems are, as a result of failing to put (1) and (2) into practice, and thus failing to put (4) into practice as well, the danger is that scientific and technological research will respond to the interests of the powerful and the wealthy, rather than to the interests of the poor, of those most in need. Scientists, officially seeking knowledge of truth *per se*, have no official grounds for objecting if those who fund research—Governments and industry—decide that the truth to be sought will reflect their interests, rather than the interests of the world's poor. And priorities of scientific research, globally, do indeed reflect the interests of the first world, rather than those of the third world.[3]

Knowledge and technology successfully pursued in a way that is not rationally subordinated to the tackling of more fundamental problems of living, through the failure to put (1), (2) and (4) into practice, is bound to lead to the kind of global problems discussed above, problems that arise as a result of newly acquired powers to act being divorced from the ability to act wisely. The creation of our current global problems, and our inability to respond adequately to these problems, has much to do, in other words, with the long-standing, rarely noticed, structural *irrationality* of our institutions and traditions of learning, devoted as they are to acquiring knowledge dissociated from learning how to tackle our problems of living in more cooperatively rational ways. Knowledge-inquiry, because of its irrationality, is designed to *intensify*, not help *solve*, our current global problems.[4]

Wisdom-inquiry

Inquiry devoted primarily to the pursuit of knowledge is, then, grossly and damagingly irrational when judged from the standpoint of contributing to human welfare by intellectual means. At once the question arises: What would a kind of inquiry be like that is devoted, in a genuinely rational way, to promoting human welfare by intellectual means? I shall call such a hypothetical kind of inquiry *wisdom-inquiry*, to stand in contrast to knowledge-inquiry.

As a first step at characterizing wisdom-inquiry, we may take knowledge-inquiry (at its best) and modify it just sufficiently to ensure that all four elementary rules of rational problem-solving, indicated above, are built into its intellectual and institutional structure: see Figure 1.

The primary change that needs to be made is to ensure that academic inquiry implements Rules 1 and 2. It becomes the fundamental task of social inquiry and the humanities (1) to articulate, and seek to improve the articulation of, our problems of living, and (2) to propose and critically assess possible solutions, from the standpoint of their practicality and desirability. In particular, social inquiry has the task of discovering how conflicts may be resolved in less violent, more cooperatively rational ways. It also has the task of

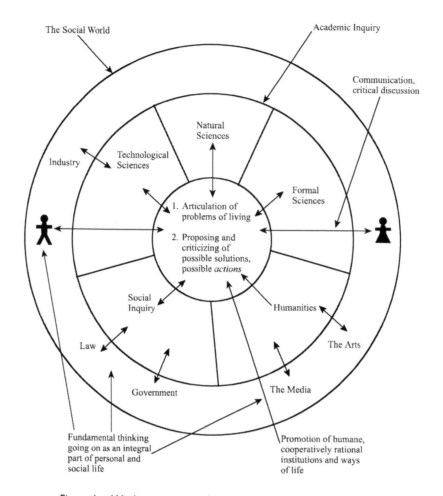

Figure I.   Wisdom-inquiry implementing problem-solving rationality

promoting such tackling of problems of living in the social world beyond academe. Social inquiry is, thus, not primarily social *science*, nor, primarily, concerned to acquire knowledge of the social world; its primary task is to promote more cooperatively rational tackling of problems of living in the social world. Pursued in this way, social inquiry is intellectually more fundamental than the natural and technological sciences, which tackle subordinate problems of knowledge, understanding and technology, in accordance with Rule 3. In Figure I, implementation of Rule 3 is represented by the specialized problem-solving of the natural, technological and formal sciences, and more specialized aspects of social inquiry and the humanities. Rule 4 is represented by the two-way arrows linking fundamental and specialized problem-solving, each influencing the other.

One can go further. According to this view, the thinking that we engage in as we live, in seeking to realize what is of value to us, is intellectually more fundamental than the whole of academic inquiry (which has, as its basic purpose, to help cooperative rational thinking and problem-solving in life to flourish). Academic thought emerges as a kind of specialization of personal and social thinking in life, the result of implementing Rule 3; this means there needs to be a two-way interplay of ideas, arguments and experiences between the social world and academia, in accordance with Rule 4. This is represented, in Figure 1, by the two-way arrows linking academic inquiry and the social world.[5]

The natural and technological sciences need to recognize three domains of discussion: evidence, theory, and aims. Discussion of aims seeks to identify that highly problematic region of overlap between that which is discoverable, and that which it is of value to discover. Discussion of what it is of value to discover interacts with social inquiry, in accordance with Rule 4.

It may be asked: but if academic inquiry today really does suffer from the wholesale structural irrationality just indicated, when and how did this come about? I turn now to a consideration of that question. The answer leads to an improved version of wisdom-inquiry, and to a new argument in support of my claim that wisdom-inquiry, potentially, is more rigorous and of greater human value, than knowledge-inquiry.

The traditional Enlightenment

The irrationality of contemporary academic inquiry has its roots in blunders made by the *philosophes* of the eighteenth century Enlightenment.

A basic idea of the Enlightenment, perhaps *the* basic idea, was to try to learn from scientific progress how to go about making social progress towards an enlightened world. The *philosophes*, Voltaire, Diderot, Condorcet and others, did what they could to put this immensely important idea into practice, in their lives. They fought dictatorial power, superstition, and injustice with weapons no more lethal than those of argument and wit. They gave their support to the virtues of tolerance, openness to doubt, readiness to learn from criticism and from experience. Courageously and energetically they laboured to promote rationality in personal and social life (Gay, 1973).

Unfortunately, in developing the Enlightenment idea intellectually, the *philosophes* blundered. They thought the task was to develop the social sciences alongside the natural sciences. I shall call this the traditional Enlightenment Programme. It was developed throughout the nineteenth century, by Comte, Marx, Mill and others, and built into the institutional structure of universities during the twentieth century, with the creation of departments of social science (see Aron, 1968, 1970; Hayek, 1979; Farganis, 1993, Introduction). Knowledge-inquiry, as we have it today, by and large, is the result, both natural science and social inquiry being devoted, in the first instance, to the pursuit of knowledge.

But, from the standpoint of creating a kind of inquiry designed to help humanity learn how to become civilized, all this amounts to a series of monumental blunders. These blunders are at the root of the damaging irrationality of current academic inquiry.

The new Enlightenment

In order to implement properly the basic Enlightenment idea of learning from scientific progress how to achieve social progress towards a civilized world, it is essential to get the following three steps right.

1. The progress-achieving methods of science need to be correctly identified.
2. These methods need to be correctly generalized so that they become fruitfully applicable to any human endeavour, whatever the aims may be, and are not just applicable to the endeavour of improving knowledge.
3. The correctly generalized progress-achieving methods then need to be exploited correctly in the great human endeavour of trying to make social progress towards an enlightened, wise, civilized world.

Unfortunately, the *philosophes* of the Enlightenment got all three points wrong. And as a result these blunders, undetected and uncorrected, are built into the intellectual–institutional structure of academia as it exists today.[6]

First, the *philosophes* failed to capture correctly the progress-achieving methods of natural science. From D'Alembert in the eighteenth century to Popper in the twentieth (Popper, 1963), the widely held view, amongst both scientists and philosophers, has been (and continues to be) that science proceeds by assessing theories impartially in the light of evidence, *no permanent assumption being accepted by science about the universe independently of evidence.* But this standard empiricist view is untenable. If taken literally, it would instantly bring science to a standstill. For, given any accepted theory of physics, T, Newtonian theory say, or quantum theory, endlessly many empirically more successful rivals can be concocted which agree with T about observed phenomena but disagree arbitrarily about some unobserved phenomena. Physics would be drowned in an ocean of such empirically more successful rival theories.

In practice, these rivals are excluded because they are disastrously disunified. *Two considerations govern acceptance of theories in physics: empirical success and unity.* But in persistently accepting unified theories, to the extent of rejecting disunified rivals that are just as, or even more, empirically successful, physics makes a big persistent assumption about the universe. The universe is such that all disunified theories are false. It has some kind of unified dynamic structure. It is physically comprehensible in the sense that explanations for phenomena exist to be discovered.

But this untestable (and thus metaphysical) assumption that the universe is comprehensible is profoundly problematic. Science is obliged to assume, but does not know, that the universe is comprehensible. Much less does it know that the universe is comprehensible in this or that way. A glance at the history of physics reveals that ideas have changed dramatically over time. In the seventeenth century there was the idea that the universe consists of corpuscles, minute billiard balls, which interact only by contact. This gave way to the idea that the universe consists of point-particles surrounded by rigid, spherically symmetrical fields of force, which in turn gave way to the idea that there is one unified self-interacting field, varying smoothly throughout space and time. Nowadays we have the idea that everything is made up of minute quantum strings embedded in 10 or 11 dimensions of space-time. Some kind of assumption along these lines must be made but, given the historical record, and given that any such assumption concerns the ultimate nature of the universe, that of which we are most ignorant, it is only reasonable to conclude that it is almost bound to be false.

The way to overcome this fundamental dilemma inherent in the scientific enterprise is to construe physics as making a hierarchy of metaphysical assumptions concerning the comprehensibility and knowability of the universe, these assumptions asserting less and less as one goes up the hierarchy, and thus becoming more and more likely to be true: see Figure 2. In this way a framework of relatively insubstantial, unproblematic, fixed assumptions and associated methods is created within which much more substantial and problematic assumptions and associated methods can be changed, and indeed improved, as scientific knowledge improves. Put another way, a framework of relatively unspecific, unproblematic, fixed *aims* and methods is created within which much more specific and problematic aims and methods evolve as scientific knowledge evolves. (A basic aim of science is to discover in what precise way the universe is comprehensible, this aim evolving as assumptions about comprehensibility evolve.) There is positive feedback between improving knowledge, and improving aims-and-methods, improving knowledge-about-how-to-improve-knowledge. This is the nub of scientific rationality, the method-ological key to the unprecedented success of science.[7] Science adapts its nature to what it discovers about the nature of the universe (see Maxwell, 1974, 1976, 1984, 1998, 2004, 2005).

So much for the first blunder of the traditional Enlightenment, and how to put it right.

Second, having failed to identify the methods of science correctly, the *philosophes* natu-rally failed to generalize these methods properly. They failed to appreciate that the idea of representing the problematic aims (and associated methods) of science in the form of a hierarchy can be generalized and applied fruitfully to other worthwhile enterprises besides science. Many other enterprises have problematic aims—problematic because aims conflict, and because what we seek may be unrealizable, undesirable, or *both*. Such enter-prises, with problematic aims, would benefit from employing a hierarchical methodology, generalized from that of science, thus making it possible to improve aims and methods as the enterprise proceeds. There is the hope that, as a result of exploiting in life methods generalized from those employed with such success in science, some of the astonishing success of science might be exported into other worthwhile human endeavours, with problematic aims quite different from those of science.

Third, and most disastrously of all, the *philosophes* failed completely to try to apply such generalized, hierarchical progress-achieving methods to the immense, and profoundly problematic enterprise of making social progress towards an enlightened, wise world. The aim of such an enterprise is notoriously problematic. For all sorts of reasons, what constitutes a good world, an enlightened, wise or civilized world, attainable and genuinely desirable, must be inherently and permanently problematic.[8] Here, above all, it is essential to employ the generalized version of the hierarchical, progress-achieving methods of science, designed specifically to facilitate progress when basic aims are problematic: see Figure 3. It is just this that the *philosophes* failed to do. Instead of applying the hierarchical methodology to *social life*, the *philosophes* sought to apply a seriously defective conception of scientific method to *social science*, to the task of making progress towards, not a *better world*, but to better *knowledge* of social phenomena. And this ancient blunder is still built into the institutional and intellectual structure of academia today, inherent in the current character of social science (Maxwell, 1984, 2007, chapters 3, 6 and 7).

Properly implemented, in short, the Enlightenment idea of learning from scientific progress how to achieve social progress towards an enlightened world would involve

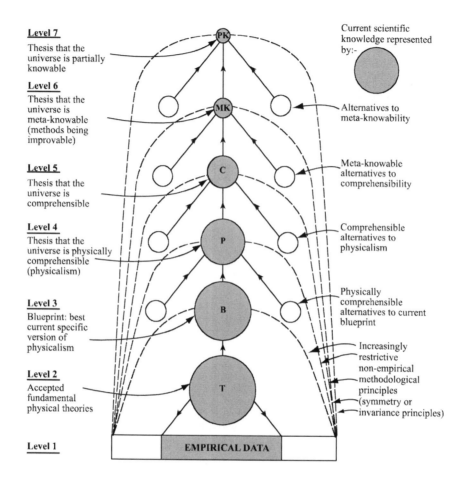

Figure 2.   Hierarchical conception of science

developing social inquiry, not as social *science*, but as social *methodology,* or social *philoso-phy.* A basic task would be to get into personal and social life, and into other institutions besides that of science—into Government, industry, agriculture, commerce, the media, law, education, international relations—hierarchical, progress-achieving methods (designed to improve problematic aims) arrived at by generalizing the methods of science. A basic task for academic inquiry as a whole would be to help humanity learn how to resolve its conflicts and problems of living in more just, cooperatively rational ways than at present. This task would be intellectually more fundamental than the scientific task of acquiring knowledge. Social inquiry would be intellectually more fundamental than physics.

As I have already remarked, academia would be a kind of people's civil service, doing openly for the public what actual civil services are supposed to do in secret for Governments. Academia would have just sufficient power (but no more) to retain its independence from Government, industry, the press, public opinion, and other centres of power and influence in the social world. It would seek to learn from, educate, and argue with the great social world beyond, but would not dictate. Academic thought would be pursued as a specialized, subordinate part of what is really important and fundamental: the thinking that goes on, individually, socially and institutionally, in the social world, guiding individual, social and institutional actions and life. The fundamental intellectual and humanitarian aim of inquiry would be to help humanity acquire wisdom—wisdom being the capacity to realize (apprehend and create) what is of value in life, for oneself and others, wisdom thus including knowledge and technological know-how but much else besides.

One outcome of getting into social and institutional life the kind of aim-evolving, hierarchical methodology indicated above, generalized from science, is that it becomes possible for us to develop and assess rival philosophies of life as a part of social life, somewhat as theories are developed and assessed within science. Such a hierarchical methodology provides a framework within which competing views about what our aims and methods in life should be—competing religious, political and moral views—may be cooperatively assessed and tested against broadly agreed, unspecific aims (high up in the hierarchy of aims) and the experience of personal and social life. There is the possibility of cooperatively and progressively improving *such philosophies of life* (views about what is of value in

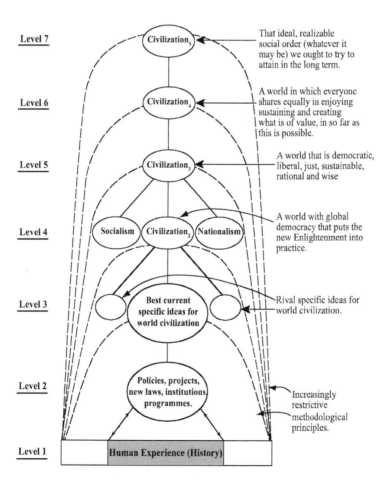

Figure 3.   Hierarchical social methodology generalized from science

life and how it is to be achieved) much as *theories* are cooperatively and progressively improved in science.

In science, ideally, theories are critically assessed with respect to each other, with respect to metaphysical ideas concerning the comprehensibility of the universe, and with respect to *experience* (observational and experimental results). In a somewhat analogous way, diverse philosophies of life may be critically assessed with respect to each other, with respect to relatively uncontroversial, agreed ideas about aims and what is of value, and with respect to *experience*— what we do, achieve, fail to achieve, enjoy and suffer—the aim being to improve philosophies of life (and more specific philosophies of more specific enterprises within life such as Government, education or art) so that they offer greater help with the realization of what is of value in life. This hierarchical methodology is especially relevant to the task of resolving conflicts about aims and ideals, as it helps disentangle agreement (high up in the hierarchy) and disagreement (more likely to be low down in the hierarchy).

Wisdom-inquiry, because of its greater rigour, has intellectual standards that are, in important respects, different from those of knowledge-inquiry. Whereas knowledge-inquiry demands that emotions and desires, values, human ideals and aspirations, philosophies of life be excluded from the intellectual domain of inquiry, wisdom-inquiry requires that they be included. In order to discover what is of value in life it is essential that we attend to our feelings and desires. But not everything we desire is desirable, and not everything that feels good is good. Feelings, desires and values need to be subjected to critical scrutiny. And of course feelings, desires and values must not be permitted to influence judgements of factual truth and falsity. Wisdom-inquiry embodies a synthesis of traditional rationalism and romanticism. It includes elements from both, and it improves on both. It incorporates romantic ideals of integrity, having to do with motivational and emotional honesty, honesty about desires and aims; and at the same time it incorporates traditional rationalist ideals of integrity, having to do with respect for objective fact, knowledge, and valid argument. Traditional rationalism takes its inspiration from science and method; romanticism takes its inspiration from art, from imagination, and from passion. Wisdom-inquiry holds art to have a fundamental rational role in inquiry, in revealing what is of value, and unmasking false values; but science, too, is of fundamental importance. What we need, for wisdom, is an interplay of sceptical rationality and emotion, an interplay of mind and heart, so that we may develop mindful hearts and heartfelt minds. It is time we healed the great rift in our culture, so graphically depicted by Snow (1986).

All in all, if the Enlightenment revolution had been carried through properly, the three steps indicated above being correctly implemented, the outcome would have been a kind of academic inquiry very different from what we have at present, inquiry devoted primarily to the intellectual aim of acquiring knowledge.

Cultural implications of wisdom-inquiry

Wisdom-inquiry does not just do better justice to the social or practical dimension of inquiry than knowledge-inquiry; it does better justice to the 'intellectual' or 'cultural' aspects as well.

From the standpoint of the intellectual or cultural aspect of inquiry, what really matters is the desire that people have to see, to know, to understand, the passionate curiosity that individuals have about aspects of the world, and the knowledge and understanding that people acquire and share as a result of actively following up their curiosity. An important task for academic thought in universities is to encourage non-professional thought to flourish outside universities. As Einstein once remarked:

> Knowledge exists in two forms—lifeless, stored in books, and alive in the consciousness of men. The second form of existence is after all the essential one; the first, indispensable as it may be, occupies only an inferior position. (Einstein, 1973, p. 80)

Wisdom-inquiry is designed to promote all this in a number of ways. It does so as a result of holding thought, at its most fundamental, to be the personal thinking we engage in as we live. It does so by recognizing that acquiring knowledge and understanding involves articulating and solving personal problems that one encounters in seeking to know and understand. It does so by recognizing that passion, emotion and desire, have a rational role to play in inquiry, disinterested research being a myth. Again, as Einstein has put it:

> The most beautiful experience we can have is the mysterious. It is the fundamental emotion which stands at the cradle of true art and true science. Whoever does not know it and can no longer wonder, no longer marvel, is as good as dead, and his eyes are dimmed. (Einstein, 1973, p. 11)

Knowledge-inquiry, by contrast, all too often fails to nourish 'the holy curiosity of inquiry' (Einstein, 1949, p. 17), and may even crush it out altogether. Knowledge-inquiry gives no rational role to emotion and desire; passionate curiosity, a sense of mystery, of wonder, have no place, officially, within the rational pursuit of knowledge. The intellectual domain becomes impersonal and split off from personal feelings and desires; it is difficult for 'holy curiosity' to flourish in such circumstances. Knowledge-inquiry hardly encourages the view that inquiry at its most fundamental is the thinking that goes on as a part of life; on the contrary, it upholds the idea that fundamental research is highly esoteric, conducted by physicists in contexts remote from ordinary life. Even though the aim of inquiry may, officially, be *human* knowledge, the personal and social dimension of this is all too easily lost sight of, and progress in knowledge is conceived of in impersonal terms, stored lifelessly in books and journals. Rare is it for popular books on science to take seriously the task of exploring the fundamental problems of a science in as accessible, non-technical and intellectually responsible a way as possible.[9] Such work is not highly regarded by knowledge-inquiry, as it does not contribute to 'expert knowledge'.

The failure of knowledge-inquiry to take seriously the highly problematic nature of the aims of inquiry leads to insensitivity as to what aims are being pursued, to a kind of institutional hypocrisy. Officially, knowledge is being sought 'for its own sake', but actually the goal may be immortality, fame, the flourishing of one's career or research group, as the existence of bitter priority disputes in science indicates. Education suffers. Science students are taught a mass of established scientific knowledge, but may not be informed of the *problems* which gave rise to this knowledge, the problems which scientists grappled with in creating the knowledge. Even more rarely are students encouraged themselves to grapple with such problems. And rare, too, is it for students to be encouraged to articulate their own problems of understanding that must, inevitably arise in absorbing all this information, or to articulate their instinctive criticisms of the received body of knowledge.

All this tends to reduce education to a kind of intellectual indoctrination, and serves to kill 'holy curiosity'.[10] Officially, courses in universities divide up into those that are vocational, like engineering, medicine and law, and those that are purely educational, like physics, philosophy or history. What is not noticed, again through insensitivity to problematic aims, is that the supposedly purely educational are actually vocational as well: the student is being trained to be an academic physicist, philosopher or historian, even though only a minute percentage of the students will go on to become academics. Real education, which must be open-ended, and without any predetermined goal, rarely exists in universities, and yet few notice. (These considerations are developed further in Maxwell, 1976, 1984, 2004.)

In order to enhance our understanding of persons as beings of value, potentially and actually, we need to understand them empathetically, by putting ourselves imaginatively into their shoes, and experiencing, in imagination, what they feel, think, desire, fear, plan, see, love and hate. For wisdom-inquiry, this kind of empathic understanding is rationally and intellectually fundamental. Articulating problems of living, and proposing and assessing possible solutions is, we have seen, the fundamental intellectual activity of wisdom-inquiry. But it is just this that we need to do to acquire empathic understanding. Social inquiry, in tackling problems of living, is also promoting empathic understanding of people. Empathic understanding is essential to wisdom. Elsewhere I have argued, indeed, that empathic understanding plays an essential role in the evolution of consciousness. It is required for cooperative action, and even for science. (For a fuller exposition of such an account of empathic understanding see Maxwell, 1984, pp. 171–189 and chapter 10; and 2001, chapters 5–7 and 9).

Granted knowledge-inquiry, on the other hand, empathic understanding hardly satisfies basic requirements for being an intellectually legitimate kind of explanation and understanding (Maxwell, 1984, pp. 183–185). It has the status merely of 'folk psychology', on a par with 'folk physics'.

Conclusion

Humanity is in trouble. We urgently need to learn how to make progress towards a wiser, more civilized world. This in turn requires that we possess traditions and institutions of learning rationally designed—*well designed*— to help us achieve this end. It is just this that we do not have at present. What we have instead is natural science and, more broadly, inquiry devoted to acquiring knowledge. Judged from the standpoint of helping us create a better world, knowledge-inquiry of this type is dangerously and damagingly irrational. We need to bring about a major intellectual and institutional revolution in the aims and methods of inquiry, from knowledge-inquiry to wisdom-inquiry. Almost every branch and aspect of academic inquiry needs to change.

A basic intellectual task of academic inquiry would be to articulate our problems of living (personal, social and global) and propose and critically assess possible solutions, possible actions. This would be the task of social inquiry and the humanities. Tackling problems of knowledge would be secondary. Social inquiry would be at the heart of the academic enterprise, intellectually more fundamental than natural science. On a rather more long-term basis, social inquiry would be concerned to help humanity build hierarchical methods of problem-solving into the fabric of social and political life so that we may gradually acquire the capacity to resolve our conflicts and problems of living in more cooperatively rational ways than at present. Natural science would change to include three domains of discussion: evidence, theory, and aims - the latter including discussion of metaphysics, values and politics. Academia would actively seek to educate the public by means of discussion and debate, and would not just study the public.

This revolution—intellectual, institutional and cultural—if it ever comes about, would be comparable in its long-term impact to that of the Renaissance, the scientific revolution, or the Enlightenment. The outcome would be traditions and institutions of learning rationally designed to help us acquire wisdom. There are a few scattered signs that this intellectual revolution, from knowledge to wisdom, is already under way. It will need, however, much wider cooperative support—from scientists, scholars, students, research councils, university administrators, vice chancellors, teachers, the media and the general public—if it is to become anything more than what it is at present, a fragmentary and often impotent movement of protest and opposition, often at odds with itself, exercising little influence on the main body of academic work. I can hardly imagine any more important work for anyone associated with academia than, in teaching, learning and research, to help promote this revolution.

Notes

1. For a much more detailed exposition of knowledge-inquiry, or 'the philosophy of knowledge', see Maxwell (1984, chapter 2). For evidence that knowledge-inquiry prevails in academia, see Maxwell (1984, chapter 6; 2000; 2007, chapter 6). I do not claim that everything in academia accords with the edicts of knowledge-inquiry. My claim is, rather, that this is the only candidate for rational inquiry in the public arena; it is the dominant view, exercising an all-pervasive influence over academe. Work that does not conform to its edicts has to struggle to survive.
2. This assumption may be challenged. Does not academic inquiry seek knowledge for its own sake—it may be asked—whether it helps promote human welfare or not? Later on, I will argue that the conception of inquiry I am arguing for, wisdom-inquiry, does better justice than knowledge-inquiry to *both* aspects of inquiry, pure and applied. The basic aim of inquiry, according to wisdom-inquiry, is to help us realize what is of value in life, 'realize' meaning both 'apprehend' and 'make real'. 'Realize' thus accommodates both aspects of inquiry, 'pure' research or 'knowledge pursued for its own sake' on the one hand, and technological or 'mission-oriented' research on the other—both, ideally, seeking to contribute to what is of value in human life. Wisdom-inquiry, like sight, is there to help us find our way around. And like sight, wisdom-inquiry is of value to us in two ways: for its intrinsic value, and for practical purposes. The first is almost more precious than the second.
3. Funds devoted, in the US, UK and some other wealthy countries, to military research are especially disturbing: see Langley (2005) and Smith (2003).
4. See Maxwell (1984, chapter 3) for a much more detailed discussion of the damaging social repercussions of knowledge-inquiry.
5. This two-way interaction between science and society is emphasized by Nowotny *et al.* (2001).

6. The blunders of the *philosophes* are not entirely undetected. Karl Popper, in his first four works, makes substantial improvements to the traditional Enlightenment programme (although Popper does not himself present his work in this fashion). Popper first improves traditional conceptions of the progress-achieving methods of science (Popper, 1959). This conception, *falsificationism*, is then generalized to become *critical rationalism*. This is then applied to social, political and philosophical problems (Popper, 1961, 1962, 1963). The version of the Enlightenment programme about to be outlined here can be regarded as a radical improvement of Popper's version: see Maxwell (2004, chapter 3).

7. Natural science has made such astonishing progress in improving knowledge and understanding of nature because it has put something like the hierarchical methodology, indicated here, into scientific practice. Officially, however, scientists continue to hold the standard empiricist view that no untestable metaphysical theses concerning the comprehensibility and knowability of the universe are accepted as a part of scientific knowledge. As I have argued elsewhere (Maxwell, 2004, chapter 2), science would be even more successful, in a number of ways, if scientists adopted and explicitly implemented the hierarchical methodology indicated here.

8. There are a number of ways of highlighting the inherently problematic character of the aim of creating civilization. People have very different ideas as to what does constitute civilization. Most views about what constitutes Utopia, an ideally civilized society, have been unrealizable *and* profoundly undesirable. People's interests, values and ideals clash. Even values that, one may hold, ought to be a part of civilization may clash. Thus freedom and equality, even though inter-related, may nevertheless clash. It would be an odd notion of individual freedom which held that freedom was for some, and not for others; and yet if equality is pursued too singlemindedly this will undermine individual freedom, and will even undermine equality, in that a privileged class will be required to enforce equality on the rest, as in the old Soviet Union. A basic aim of legislation for civilization, we may well hold, ought to be increase freedom by restricting it: this brings out the inherently problematic, paradoxical character of the aim of achieving civilization. One thinker who has stressed the inherently problematic, contradictory character of the idea of civilization is Isaiah Berlin; see, for example, Berlin (1980, pp. 74–79). Berlin thought the problem could not be solved; I, on the contrary, hold that the hierarchical methodology indicated here provides us with the means to learn how to improve our solution to it in real life.

9. A recent, remarkable exception is Penrose (2004).

10. I might add that the hierarchical conception of science indicated here does better justice to the scientific quest for understanding than does orthodox standard empiricist views: see Maxwell (1998, chapters 4 and 8; 2004, chapter 2).

Notes on contributor

Nicholas Maxwell has devoted much of his working life to arguing that we need to bring about a revolution in academia so that it seeks and promotes wisdom and does not just acquire knowledge. He has published five books on this theme, including *From Knowledge to Wisdom* (1984), *The Comprehensibility of the Universe* (1998), *The Human World in the Physical Universe* (2001) and *Is Science Neurotic?* (2004): see www.nickmaxwell.demon.co.uk. For many years he taught philosophy of science at University College London, where he is now Emeritus Reader.

References

Appleyard, B. (1992) *Understanding the present: science and the soul of modern man* (London, Picador).
Aron, R. (1968) *Main currents in sociological thought. Volume 1* (Harmondsworth, Penguin).

Aron, R. (1970) *Main currents in sociological thought. Volume 2* (Harmondsworth, Penguin).

Berlin, I. (1980) *Against the current* (London, Hogarth Press).

Berman, B. (1981) *The reenchantment of the world* (Ithaca, Cornell University Press).

Einstein, A. (1949) Autobiographical notes, in: P. A. Schilpp (Ed.) *Albert Einstein: philosopher-scientist* (Illinois, Open Court), 3–94.

Einstein, A. (1973) *Ideas and opinions* (London, Souvenir Press).

Farganis, J. (Ed.) (1993) *Readings in social theory: the classic tradition to post-modernism* (New York, McGraw-Hill).

Feyerabend, P. (1978) *Against method* (London, Verso).

Feyerabend, P. (1987) *Farewell to reason* (London, Verso).

Gay, P. (1973) *The Enlightenment: an interpretation* (London, Wildwood House).

Hayek, F. A. (1979) *The counter-revolution of science* (Indianapolis, Liberty Press).

Laing, R. D. (1965) *The divided self* (Harmondsworth, Penguin).

Langley, C. (2005) *Soldiers in the laboratory* (Folkestone, Scientists for Global Responsibility).

Marcuse, H. (1964) *One dimensional man* (Boston, Beacon Press).

Maxwell, N. (1974) The rationality of scientific discovery, *Philosophy of Science,* 41, 123–153, 247–295.

Maxwell, N. (1976) *What's wrong with science?* (Frome, Bran's Head Books).

Maxwell, N. (1980) Science, reason, knowledge and wisdom: a critique of specialism, *Inquiry,* 23, 19–81.

Maxwell, N. (1984) *From knowledge to wisdom* (Oxford, Blackwell). (2nd edn, enlarged, 2007, Pentire Press, London).

Maxwell, N. (1998) *The comprehensibility of the universe* (Oxford, Oxford University Press).

Maxwell, N. (2001) *The human world in the physical universe* (Lanham, Rowman & Littlefield).

Maxwell, N. (2004) *Is science neurotic?* (London, Imperial College Press).

Maxwell, N. (2005) Popper, Kuhn, Lakatos and aim-oriented empiricism, *Philosophia,* 32, 181–239.

Nowotny, H., Scott, P. & Gibbons, M. (2001) *Re-thinking science* (Cambridge, Polity Press).

Penrose, R. (2004) *The road to reality* (London, Jonathan Cape).

Popper, K. R. (1959) *The logic of scientific discovery* (London, Hutchinson).

Popper, K. R. (1961) *The poverty of historicism* (London, Routledge).

Popper, K. R. (1962) *The open society and its enemies* (London, Routledge).

Popper, K. R. (1963) *Conjectures and refutations* (London, Routledge).

Roszak, T. (1973) *Where the wasteland ends* (London, Faber & Faber).

Schwartz, B. (1987) *The battle for human nature* (New York, W. W. Norton).

Smith, D. (2003) *The atlas of war and peace* (London, Earthscan).

Snow, C. P. (1986) *The two cultures: and a second look* (Cambridge, Cambridge University Press)

Yeats, W. B. (1950) The second coming, in: *Collected poems* (London, Macmillan).

From knowledge-inquiry to wisdom-inquiry: is the revolution underway?

Mathew Iredale

Introduction

For more than 30 years, Nicholas Maxwell has argued that we need a revolution in the aims and methods of academic inquiry. Instead of giving priority to the search for knowledge, or knowledge-inquiry, academia should devote itself to wisdom-inquiry; seeking and promoting wisdom by rational means, wisdom being understood to mean the capacity to realize what is of value in life, for oneself and others (wisdom thus including knowledge but much else besides).

What is knowledge-inquiry? At its most basic, it is simply the search for knowledge, or truth, but in its more common, more humane form, it can best be summed up by Farrington's description of Francis Bacon's 'great idea':

> The idea is a commonplace today, partly realized, partly tarnished, still often misunderstood; but in his day it was a novelty. It is simply that knowledge ought to bear fruit in works, that science ought to be applicable to industry, that men ought to organize themselves as a sacred duty to improve and transform the conditions of life. (Farrington, 1951, p. 3)

Thus knowledge-inquiry may be characterized as having two basic aims: (1) the acquisition of knowledge; and (2) the use of that knowledge to help people, society, the environment, etc.

Maxwell is critical of knowledge-inquiry because it does not give priority to articulating, and improving the articulation of, our problems of living, and proposing and critically assessing possible solutions and possible actions. And so academic inquiry pursued in accordance with knowledge-inquiry, whilst it can often be wonderfully beneficial, can also sometimes be enormously harmful:

> It is hardly too much to say that all our current global problems have come about because of the successful scientific pursuit of knowledge and technological know-how dissociated from wisdom. The appalling destructiveness of modern warfare and terrorism, vast inequalities in wealth and standards of living between first and third worlds, rapid population growth, environmental damage—destruction of tropical rain forests, rapid extinction of species, global warming, pollution of sea, earth and air, depletion of finite natural resources—all exist today because of the massively enhanced power to act (of some), made possible by modern science and technology. Nevertheless, science as such is not the problem, but rather science dissociated from the pursuit of wisdom. (Maxwell, 2003, p. 24)

In contrast to knowledge-inquiry, wisdom-inquiry would give intellectual priority to the personal and social problems we encounter in our lives as we strive to realize what is of value, problems of knowledge and technology being intellectually subordinate. In this way, says Maxwell, wisdom-inquiry is better able to help us to resolve the global problems described above.

Aim-oriented empiricism, aim-oriented rationality and wisdom-inquiry

There is no doubt that wisdom-inquiry *has* been put into practice, at least to some degree, in ignorance of Maxwell's detailed discussion of the explicit steps needed to be taken to put it into practice. (Maxwell himself uses the example of Albert Einstein in *From knowledge to wisdom* and elsewhere.) There have always been individuals more aware of the wider implications of their work, just as there are those who only see as far as the next experiment.

Nor is there any doubt that Maxwell's ideas have, on the whole, been well received; over a 30-year period, a number of his central arguments have been endorsed by academics in a wide variety of disciplines. The philosopher George Kneller was an early and enthusiastic supporter:

> Maxwell's theory of aim-oriented empiricism is the outstanding work on scientific change since Lakatos, and his thesis is surely correct. Scientific growth should be rationally directed through the discussion, choice, and modification of aim-incorporating blueprints rather than left to haphazard competition among research traditions seeking empirical success alone. (Kneller, 1978, p. 84)

Kneller concluded that 'No other theory provides, as Maxwell's does in principle, for the rational direction of the overall growth of science' (Kneller, 1978, p. 91).

When *From knowledge to wisdom* was first published it received many favourable reviews.[1] The late Professor Christopher Longuet-Higgins, physicist, chemist and cognitive scientist, wrote a glowing review in *Nature*, concluding that 'There are altogether too many symptoms of malaise in our science-based society for Nicholas Maxwell's diagnosis to be ignored' (Longuet-Higgins, 1984, p. 204). The philosopher Mary Midgley described *From knowledge to wisdom* as 'this powerful, profound and important book' (Midgley, 1986, p. 427).

And over the years Maxwell's work has influenced scholars in a range of disciplines, including anthropology (Harris, 1979), psychology (Dixon, 1987; Chisholm, 1999; Katzko, 2004), literature (Lodge, 2002), economics (Blaug, 1980), philosophy (Harré, 1986; Midgley, 1989; Dennett, 2003), environmentalism (Burrows *et al.*, 1991), technology studies (Martin, 1997), engineering (Elms, 1989), rhetoric (Crowley, 1989) and education (Hargreaves & Hargreaves, 1983; Awbrey & Scott, 1994; Elliot, 1989, 1990).

To give some specific examples from education, John Elliott, Professor of Education within the Centre for Applied Research in Education at the University of East Anglia has explored in some detail the relationship between Maxwell's view of inquiry in general and the development of a theory of educational action research (Elliott, 1989). He also favourably mentioned Maxwell's work in his Presidential Address to the British Educational Research Association (Elliott, 1990).

In 1994, Lee Shulman, now president of The Carnegie Foundation for the Advancement of Teaching, and the late Donald Schön, of the Massachusetts Institute of Technology, both gave presentations praising Maxwell's work (especially Maxwell, 1992) to the American Association for Higher Education Conference on Faculty Roles and Rewards (Shulman, 1994; Schön, 1994). Shulman recently stated in a personal communication to the author that 'I continue to find the ideas expressed as sadly sensible'.

Susan Awbrey, now Vice-Provost for Undergraduate Education, Oakland University, and David Scott, former Chancellor of the University of Massachusetts Amherst, have also favourably discussed Maxwell's work (Awbrey & Scott, 1994) and not only agree that a revolution of the sort he describes is necessary, but that 'the university [of Massachusetts Amherst] has already begun a transformation to the philosophy of wisdom'. They go on to state:

> Essentially, Maxwell is saying that universities must move from a limiting philosophy of knowledge to a philosophy of wisdom. We believe that this broader vision must be found if we are to inhabit a world in which people are prepared and willing to deliberate about issues that affect their lives and to take responsibility for the decisions that will maintain and enhance democracy.

Unfortunately, having quoted with approval Maxwell's basic message—that problems of knowledge and understanding need to be tackled as rationally subordinate to intellectually more fundamental problems of living—the authors then decide to take quite a different tack. In considering how a change to wisdom-inquiry might impact upon their university they state that 'it is first necessary to say what one means by wisdom', even though Maxwell himself makes it abundantly clear that when talking about wisdom-inquiry, wisdom should be taken to mean the capacity to realize what is of value in life, for oneself and others. A general discussion of the meaning of wisdom is not only unnecessary, it can actually be counter-productive, as in this instance. Awbrey and Scott, having discussed several different conceptions of wisdom, settle upon one that is quite far removed from Maxwell's meaning of the term. It is based upon a seven-stage model of reflective judgement developed by Karen Kitchener and P. M. King (Kitchener & Brenner, 1990):

1. Knowledge simply exists and therefore, does not need justification.
2. Knowledge is absolutely certain, or certain but not immediately available.

3. Knowledge is absolutely certain or temporarily uncertain.
4. Knowledge is idiosyncratic since situational variables dictate that we cannot know with certainty.
5. Knowledge is contextual and subjective.
6. Knowledge is personally constructed via evaluations of evidence, opinions of others, etc, across contexts.
7. Knowledge is constructed via the process of reasonable inquiry into generalizable conjectures about the problem at hand.

Awbrey and Scott state that 'in these last stages we see the emergence of wisdom'. Maybe so, for one meaning of wisdom, but nowhere in this model does there appear to be an awareness that problems of knowledge and understanding need to be tackled as rationally subordinate to intellectually more fundamental problems of living, as Maxwell's wisdom-inquiry requires. It is just knowledge-inquiry described as wisdom-inquiry.

Consequently, when Awbrey and Scott conclude that 'To construct a university based upon the philosophy of wisdom will require us to move to stage seven of Kitchener and King's model,' they are unfortunately mistaken. Although such a move might make the University of Massachusetts Amherst a better institution, is not really moving it towards wisdom-inquiry in the way described by Maxwell.

But I do not wish to be critical, as Awbrey and Scott clearly do appreciate the importance of Maxwell's argument that there is a need fundamentally to transform academic inquiry. And this is more than can be said for most academics. Indeed, it is not an exaggeration to say that the vast body of academic work has proceeded on its way entirely unaffected by Maxwell's work. The evidence that a revolution has taken place, or is doing so, remains decidedly mixed, at least as far as the detailed steps of Maxwell's revolution are concerned.

For example, consider the situation with regard to scientific inquiry specifically. Wisdom-inquiry does not simply require scientists to be a bit more forward looking in their research; to bear in mind ethical or environmental implications, that sort of thing. Rather, it requires that science abandons the orthodox view that the intellectual aim of science is truth per se, the basic method being to assess claims to knowledge impartially with respect to the evidence. Instead, scientists need to acknowledge that the real aims of science inherently involve problematic assumptions concerning metaphysics, values and politics. Scientists then need to adopt and put into practice what Maxwell calls aim-oriented empiricism, a conception of scientific method that creates a framework of relatively unspecific, unproblematic aims and methods within which much more specific and problematic aims and methods may be improved as scientific knowledge improves. Aim-oriented empiricism can be generalized to form aim-oriented rationality, a conception of rationality specifically designed to help us achieve worthwhile, problematic aims whatever we may be doing. Here, too, a framework of relatively unspecific, unproblematic aims and associated methods is created within which much more specific and problematic aims and methods may be improved as we proceed. Finally, social inquiry and the humanities have the task of helping humanity discover how to put aim-oriented rationality into the fabric of social life, into all other institutions besides science. The outcome of all this is wisdom-inquiry.

But what this means in practice is that scientists are being asked to transform the way in which they work, and this will clearly be a very difficult thing for a successful, practising scientist to do, especially when the message is coming from a non-scientist. And I have to say more generally that I have found very little evidence that any academic or institution is trying to transform their work along the lines advocated by aim-oriented empiricism or aim-oriented rationality. However, if one takes a more general outlook, if one regards wisdom-inquiry as putting social, ethical, environmental and other *human* considerations at the very heart of academic inquiry, then many of the signs are much more favourable.

Interdisciplinary research initiatives

Over the last few years a number of interdisciplinary initiatives have been specifically set up in order to tackle some of the major social and environmental problems confronting mankind. These initiatives do not just involve research groups from different departments of the same academic institute, but research groups from different institutes.

Perhaps the most impressive example of this is the Tyndall Centre for Climate Change Research (www.tyndall.ac.uk). Founded in 2000 by 28 scientists from various different research institutes, it is based in six universities, has links with six others, and is funded by three research councils; the Natural Environment Research Council (NERC), the Engineering and Physical Sciences Research Council (EPSRC) and the Economic and Social Research Council (ESRC).

The Tyndall Centre brings together scientists, economists, engineers and social scientists, who work together to develop sustainable responses to climate change through trans-disciplinary research and dialogue on both a national and international level - not just within the research community, but also with business leaders, policy advisors, the media and the public in general.

Such inter-departmental and inter-university cooperation, to tackle global problems of living, is a vital part of the move towards wisdom-inquiry. And the Tyndall Centre is not alone in such an approach.

The UK Energy Research Centre (www.ukerc.ac.uk) was established in 2004 following a recommendation from the 2002 review of energy initiated by Sir David King, the Government's Chief Scientific Advisor. Their mission is to be the UK's pre-eminent centre of research, and source of authoritative information and leadership, on sustainable energy systems. The Energy Research Centre comprises over 80 researchers based across the UK at various universities and institutions and, like the Tyndall Centre, is funded by the EPSRC, the NERC and the ESRC.

Similar initiatives exist at both Oxford and Cambridge universities. At Cambridge, there is the Cambridge Environmental Initiative (www.cei.group.cam.ac.uk). Launched in 2004, it aims to facilitate and support interdisciplinary environmental research within the University of Cambridge and to provide research-driven colloquia to promote networking and communication between academics with related research interests. The members of the Cambridge Environmental Initiative Steering Group include representatives of each of the six academic schools in the University: Arts and Humanities, Biological Sciences, Clinical

Medicine, Humanities and Social Sciences, Physical Sciences and Technology. It is thus truly interdisciplinary.

At Oxford, there is the Oxford University Centre for the Environment (www.ouce.ox.ac.uk). Launched in 2005, it consists of the academic department of the School of Geography and two established research centres; the Environmental Change Institute and the Transport Studies Unit. There are over 30 academic staff members in the Centre engaged in research and teaching and more than 50 researchers. The Centre has strong links with both the Tyndall Centre for Climate Change Research and the UK Energy Research Centre.

Other more modest groups exist at other universities. They have been created in order to carry out research into, and so find solutions to, some of the major social and environmental problems confronting mankind. To this end, they are to some extent representative of a wisdom-based approach to inquiry.

Professional bodies

As I write, work is currently underway to produce the third edition of *On being a scientist: responsible conduct in research* (second edition available online at http://books.nap.edu/readingroom/books/obas/). First published by the Washington-based National Academy of Sciences in 1989, and updated in 1995, *On being a scientist* sought to describe the ethical foundations of scientific practices and some of the personal and professional issues that researchers encountered in their work.

It cannot be denied that the booklet concentrates on the responsibilities of scientists for the advancement of science—chapter headings include 'Conflicts of interest', 'Misconduct in science' and 'Responding to violations of ethical standards'—but there is also recognition that scientists have additional responsibilities to society:

> Even scientists conducting the most fundamental research need to be aware that their work can ultimately have a great impact on society. Construction of the atomic bomb and the development of recombinant DNA—events that grew out of basic research on the nucleus of the atom and investigations of certain bacterial enzymes, respectively—are two examples of how seemingly arcane areas of science can have tremendous societal consequences.

However, although the booklet states clearly that if they find that their discoveries have implications for some important aspect of public affairs, scientists have a responsibility to call attention to the public issues involved, it falls short of suggesting that scientists might consider curtailing or abandoning their work if it has unwanted implications or recognizing that the public can play an active part in helping to articulate the aims and methods of science. It clearly puts the science first, and society second, and as such is more oriented towards knowledge-inquiry than wisdom-inquiry. Whether the third edition will expand upon the role of the scientist in society, time will tell.

If it did, it would certainly bring it more into line with current thinking at other scientific bodies, such as the British Association for the Advancement of Science and The Royal Society. There are elements of wisdom-inquiry in the recent Presidential Addresses of both organizations. The British Association's President for 2004–2005 was Professor

Robert Winston and he used his Presidential Address (available online at www.the-ba.net/
the-ba/Events/FestivalofScience/FestivalNews/_BAPresidentialAddress2005.htm) to discuss
the future of science and the role of the scientist in society. Throughout the address, he
emphasizes the social nature of science. He begins by making the point that 'whether
scientists like it or not, technological advance is now increasingly seen as a massive
threat—to mankind, and to our planet. And rightly'. In other words, a clear recognition of
the problems which arise from science pursued in accordance with knowledge-inquiry.

He goes on to criticize the direction in which science is being pushed by the
Government:

> We have recently seen that the UK Government is committed to scientific research because
> it is convinced that it will make Britain more economically competitive. ... In the UK,
> economic reasons seem almost entirely the only stated reason for the increased funding—
> science is seen as a financial investment. ... Science is no longer seen as an essential part of
> our culture or as an important expression of essential human inquisitiveness.

In other words, the essential social element of science is being compromised for the
sake of economic considerations. But it is this social element that is vital for science, says
Winton. Scientists need to take greater notice of public concerns, and relate and react to
them. He argues that the time is right for academically examining the means and the details
of public engagement. He describes a recent publication from the UK think tank, Demos,
which has argued the case for so-called 'upstream public engagement'. It recently
suggested that lay members of the public should be much more involved in deciding which
scientific research is done and how it is conducted, something which is at the very heart of
wisdom-inquiry.

Winston is also not afraid to admit that many people do not consider that scientists
take the ethical implications of their work seriously enough. As the geneticist Elof Axel
Carlson recently noted: 'Scientists sometimes argue that their job is to solve the technical
or scientific problems, and it is not their responsibility how that knowledge is put to use'
(Carlson, 2006, p. 15). For Winston, this is unacceptable; ethical considerations should be
a fundamental part of science (which is another element of wisdom-inquiry):

> Nowhere are science undergraduates routinely taught ethics. Few budding scientists and engi-
> neers have formal training in thinking about the public implications of what they are learning.
> My impression, in lecturing and giving seminars in many British and overseas universities, is
> that young scientists are eager to understand the ethical aspects of the technology for which
> they may be responsible. ... Every university teaching science should include compulsory
> modules which are concerned with the ethics of conducting science and the consequences of
> not considering the social implications of new technology.

Winston ends his address with a number of 'challenges for scientists'. There are several
that are relevant to wisdom-inquiry. In the first challenge, Winston makes the point that
sometimes the public may be absolutely right that the technology that scientists create is
not to be fully trusted and that scientists need to accept this. New technologies can
undoubtedly lead societies into danger, and scientists need to be more modest in openly
accepting these risks. In Challenge 5, Winston states that scientists need to help Governments to research how much engagement contributes to public trust and what are the
best ways of conducting it: 'If the public truly owns science, then we have a duty to find

out how they want to use it'. And in Challenge 7 he states simply that 'Scientists need to be educated in ethics and demonstrate more understanding of ethical issues'.

Several of the points made by Professor Winston are also to be found in Lord May's 2005 Anniversary Address to the Royal Society (available online at www.royalsoc.ac.uk/publication.asp?year=2005&id=2181). May begins by arguing that the advances in scientific understanding that are the legacy of the 'deliberately experimental and fact-based Enlightenment' have resulted in today's world being 'the best of times and the worst of times'. It is the best of times because we are healthier, better fed, and with more energy subsidies than ever before; it is the worst of times because the well-intentioned actions that gave us better health, more food and more energy all have unintended adverse consequences, which we are only just beginning fully to appreciate. (For Maxwell, this is at least partly as a result of science being pursued in accordance with knowledge-inquiry.)

May's next point is most interesting. He argues that because the problems that we face are global in nature, 'the involvement of the scientific community—in basic understanding, in practical measures, and in policy recommendations—needs to transcend national boundaries'.

In saying that scientists have a significant role to play in the resolution of these problems, there is the clear recognition that science is part of the cause. This is a notable change from the past, when scientists were ready to accept praise for the good things that came from science, and yet quick to deny blame for the bad, putting the blame instead upon certain individuals or humanity in general. Carlson again:

> Some scientists walk away from personal responsibility, believing that they only provided the know-how and were not authorized to make the decisions that harmed others. That is generally true for those whose research is not intentionally applied and who were only seeking to understand nature. It is almost certainly false for those who work to apply science for human use. (Carlson, 2006, p. 16)

May's address is further evidence of the growing appreciation by scientists that science is very much a part of society, and can contribute both good and bad to that society. This is best illustrated by the following passage:

> In everything I have said above there is the implicit, but hugely important, assumption that the scientific community has an obligation to explain itself—its agenda, its achievements, and their potential applications—to the public. This means individual scientists engaging more with wider society, explaining what they do and why, and responding through dialogue and debate to the interests, concerns and aspirations of the public. Such engagement is not always easy, in part because it often requires simplifying things (usually painful to researchers for whom the details can be entrancing), and must always avoid distortion. This dialogue between researchers and the general public—or, more accurately, the many and varied 'publics'—has in recent years been seen as an integral part of the scientific process. The UK has, I believe, been a leader in this, partly as the result of unfortunate earlier experiences (BSE in particular). The Royal Society hopes that, through its 'Science in Society' programme and other activities, it has been creative in its exploration of such engagement.

As was mentioned earlier, active involvement of the public in scientific research is at the heart of wisdom-inquiry and the Science in Society programme to which May refers (available online at www.royalsoc.ac.uk/page.asp?id=1988) is a significant step towards achieving this. The programme was set up by The Royal Society in 2000 in response to controversies over BSE and genetically modified foods. It has five main aims:

1. To develop a widespread, innovative and effective system of dialogue with society.
2. To involve society positively in influencing and sharing responsibility for policy on scientific matters.
3. To embrace a culture of openness in decision-making.
4. To take account of the values and attitudes of the public.
5. To enable the Society to promote the national science policy.

It can be seen from these aims, and especially Aims 1, 2 and 4, that if the Science in Society programme gains widespread acceptance by scientists, and is acted upon, it could help to bring about a significant shift from knowledge-inquiry towards wisdom-inquiry.

Pressure groups

The examples above are from what may be regarded as the official representatives of science; the National Academy of Sciences, the Royal Society and the British Association. But what of more unofficial representatives?

The International Network of Engineers and Scientists for Global Responsibility (www.inesglobal.com) is an independent non-profit organization concerned about the impact of science and technology on society. The INESGR was founded in 1991 and now has a network of over 90 member organizations and individual members in 40 countries. They have recognized for some time the important point only recently been voiced by the scientific establishment in Britain (in the Presidential Addresses of Lords Winston and May), that engineers and scientists have played a key role both in the processes that threaten international security and those that provide hope for the future. They aim to encourage and facilitate international communication among engineers and scientists seeking to promote international peace and security, justice and sustainable development and working for a responsible use of science and technology. To this end, they work for the reduction of military spending and for the transfer of resources to the satisfaction of basic needs, promote environmentally sound technologies while taking long-term effects into account, and raise the awareness of ethical principles among engineers and scientists and to support those who have been victimized for acting upon such principles.

A similar group is Scientists for Global Responsibility (www.sgr.org.uk), a UK-based organization which was formed in 1992 from several smaller organizations which had all been set up to campaign to reduce the widespread use of science and technology for military purposes. The break-up of the Soviet Union and the end of the Cold War lead to the organizations deciding to merge and widen their focus. A general concern about the misuse of science and technology in threatening human life and the wider environment became their central aim.

Like the INESGR, Scientists for Global Responsibility have recognized and publicly stated that many of the problems facing society today are as a result of science and technology and that this has lead people to become disillusioned with science and technology. They too stress the social nature of science, the importance of promoting constructive dialogue between scientists and non-scientists, and that any problems that arise from science and technology will require a combination of scientific, economic and political solutions.

There are various areas of our lives that they believe would benefit from more science and technology funding: the clean, sustainable production of energy, and its efficient use; the development and application of biological and medical knowledge to the benefit of all; the study of social and economic affairs with the aim of improving the lot of all; and the use of information technology to increase energy efficiency, reduce the need for transportation, eliminate unnecessary labour, and promote access for all to humanity's pool of knowledge.

All of these points can be seen as aspects of wisdom-inquiry, in that they acknowledge the social nature of science, call for science to be more open in its work and to explicitly target its work for the benefit of mankind.

The same can be said of another, more recent, group, The Independent Science Panel (www.indsp.org). Founded in 2003, they comprise some 30 scientists from a variety of disciplines who are committed to 'the Promotion of Science for the Public Good'. They believe that science should be accountable to civil society and that all sectors of civil society should participate in making decisions on all issues related to science, from scientific research to policies regarding science and technologies. They also hold that science should contribute to the physical, social and spiritual well-being of all in all societies and they reject scientific endeavours that serve aggressive military ends, promote commercial imperialism or damage social justice.

By bringing together like-minded scientists from a wide variety of backgrounds, engaging the public, and creating media attention, these pressure groups are perhaps even more representative of wisdom-inquiry than the research groups mentioned earlier, such as the Tyndall Centre and the Cambridge Environmental Initiative. Whether they will be able to affect real change, or be viewed as mere fringe groups to the official scientific bodies, remains to be seen, although they do enjoy the support of some heavyweight scientists and academics.

Is the revolution underway?

What this discussion has shown is that there are reasonable grounds to be optimistic that wisdom-inquiry, in the general sense of putting social, ethical, environmental and other *human* considerations at the very heart of academic inquiry, is taking place to some degree.

Specifically, we can make the following points:

1. There is now a clear admission amongst scientists that many of the problems facing society today are as a result of science and technology.
2. It is recognized by academics that a multidisciplinary approach, both inter-departmental and inter-university, is necessary to solve the problems that face mankind and, more importantly, key steps have been taken to put this approach into practice.
3. The scientific community has realized that in promoting the public understanding of science, the communication should not just go from scientist to public. There appears

to be a genuine appreciation that a two way dialogue is both desirable and necessary and that scientists can and must learn from the public.

4. Related to Point 4, there is a clear understanding of and emphasis upon the social nature of science.

5. There is a recognition of the importance of teaching ethics to scientists, and not just those involved in medical or applied sciences, but all scientists.

As far as Maxwell's more specific hopes for wisdom-inquiry are concerned—that there needs to be a fundamental reorganization of academic inquiry so that it gives priority to articulating, and improving the articulation of, our problems of living, and proposing and critically assessing possible solutions and possible actions—the evidence is less optimistic. Indeed, in this regard, things do not seem to have moved on appreciably in the last twenty years.

But perhaps this should come as no surprise. When a man calls for a revolution, and not just a revolution in the aims and methods of something as complex and specialized as science, but a revolution in the aims and methods of the whole of academic inquiry, it is easy to find reasons to be dismissive. Even if one understands what is being called for—a comprehensive intellectual revolution, affecting to a greater or lesser extent all branches of academic inquiry—and even if one agrees with the need for such a revolution, one may despair at the enormity of the task ahead.

One may argue that academic inquiry is too well entrenched in its ways to change, that scientific inquiry is too powerful and successful to contemplate the notion that there is a fundamental error at the very heart of scientific inquiry, or that scientists will be too quick to conclude that this is yet another attempt to discredit science, to possibly contemplate the revolution in question. Individual academics may occasionally offer informal approval of the need for a revolution of the sort in question, or of parts of the revolution, but academia as a whole will not change, will not see the need to change, and will resist calls for such a change with all their might.

But such a reaction would be unwarranted. What we have seen is that parts of the academic community can change, that they can recognize where they have gone wrong before and appreciate the need to change the way they work in the future. And as such, more clearly than ever one can see the beginnings of a shift from knowledge-inquiry to wisdom-inquiry.

Acknowledgements

I wish to thank the two anonymous referees for their helpful comments on an earlier draft of this paper.

Notes

1. For favourable reviews of Maxwell (1984) see Collingridge (1985), Easlea (1986), Foss (1986), and Richards (1985); for Maxwell (1998) see Chakravartty (1999), Juhl (2000), Muller (2004), Roush (2001), Shanks (2000) and Smart (2000); for Maxwell (2001) see Hodgson (2002) and Newton (2003); and for Maxwell (2004) see Grebovicz (2006), Iredale (2005), Schiff (2005), McHenry (2006) and McNiven (2005).

Notes on contributor

Mathew Iredale is based in London and has written the Sci Phi column for *The Philosophers'
Magazine* for the last nine years. He studied human sciences and then history and
philosophy of science before taking a Ph.D. in philosophy of science at University
College London.

References

Awbrey, S. M. & Scott, D. K. (1994) *Knowledge into wisdom: unveiling inherent values and beliefs to construct a
    wise university.* Available online at: www.umass.edu/pastchancellors/scott/papers/knowWisdom.html
    (accessed 28 February 2007).
Blaug, M. (1980) *The methodology of economics* (Cambridge, Cambridge University Press).
Burrows, B., Mayne, A. & Newbury P. (1991) *Into the twenty-first century* (London, Adamantine Press).
Carlson, E. A. (2006) *Times of triumph, times of doubt: science and the battle for public trust* (New York, Cold
    Spring Harbor Laboratory Press).
Chakravartty, A. (1999, September 24) Physics, metaphysics, *Times Higher Education Supplement*, p. 24.
Chisholm, J. (1999) *Death, hope and sex* (Cambridge, Cambridge University Press).
Collingridge, D. (1985) Reforming science, *Social Studies of Science*, 15, 763–769.
Committee on Science Engineering and Public Policy (1995) *On being a scientist: responsible conduct in research.*
    Available online at: http://books.nap.edu/readingroom/books/obas/ (accessed 28 February 2007).
Crowley, S. (1989) A plea for the revival of sophistry, *Rhetoric Review*, 7(2), 318–334.
Dennett, D. (2003) *Freedom evolves* (London, Allen Lane).
Dixon, N. F. (1987) *Our own worst enemy* (London, Futura).
Easlea, B. (1986) Review of 'From knowledge to wisdom: a revolution in the aims and methods of science'
    by Nicholas Maxwell, *Journal of Applied Philosophy*, 3, 139–140.
Elliott, J. (1989) Educational theory and the professional learning of teachers: an overview, *Cambridge
    Journal of Education*, 19, 81–102.
Elliott, J. (1990) Educational research in crisis: performance indicators and the decline in excellence
    (BERA Presidential Address), *British Educational Research Journal*, 16(1), 3–18.
Elms, D. G. (1989) Wisdom engineering, *Journal of Applied Engineering Education*, 5(6), 711–717.
Farrington, B. (1951) *Francis Bacon: philosopher of industrial science* (London, Lawrence & Wishart).
Foss, J. (1986) Review of 'From knowledge to wisdom: a revolution in the aims and methods of science'
    by Nicholas Maxwell, *Canadian Philosophical Reviews*, 6(5), 235–237.
Grebowicz, M. (2006) 'Where have the philosophers been all this time?' Reading Maxwell's revolution,
    Metascience, 15, 141–144.
Hargreaves, J. & Hargreaves, T. (1983) Some models of school science in British curriculum projects,
    Social Studies of Science, 13(4), 569–604.
Harré, R. (1986) *Varieties of realism* (Oxford, Blackwell).
Harris, M. (1980) *Cultural materialism* (New York, Vintage).
Hodgson, D. (2002) Review of 'The human world in the physical universe' by Nicholas Maxwell, *Journal of
    Consciousness Studies*, 9, 93–94.
Iredale, M. (2005) Review of is science neurotic?, *The Philosophers' Magazine*, 31, 86–87.
Juhl, C. F. (2000) Review of 'The Comprehensibility of the Universe: a new conception of science' by
    Nicholas Maxwell, *International Philosophical Quarterly*, XL(4), 517–518.
Katzko, M. (2004) Pyschology's dilemma: an institutional neurosis?, *Journal of Clinical Psychology*, 60(12),
    1237–1241.
Kneller, G. (1978) *Science as a human endeavor* (New York, Columbia University Press).
Lodge, D. (2002) *Consciousness and the novel* (London, Secker & Warburg).
Longuet-Higgins, C. (1984) For goodness sake, *Nature*, 312, p. 204.
Martin, B. (1997) Science, technology and nonviolent action, *Social Studies of Science*, 27(3), 439–463.

Maxwell, N. (1976) *What's wrong with science?* (Hayes, Bran's Head Books).

Maxwell, N. (1984) *From knowledge to wisdom: a revolution in the aims and methods of science* (Oxford, Basil Blackwell).

Maxwell, N. (1992) What kind of inquiry can best help us create a good world?, *Science, Technology and Human Values,* 17(2), 205–227.

Maxwell, N. (1998) *The comprehensibility of the universe* (Oxford, Oxford University Press).

Maxwell, N. (2001) *The human world in the physical universe* (Lanham, Rowman & Littlefield).

Maxwell, N. (2003) Do philosophers love wisdom, *The Philosophers' Magazine,* 22, 22–24.

Maxwell, N. (2004) *Is science neurotic?* (London, Imperial College Press).

May, R. (2005) Threats to tomorrow's world, *Anniversary Address to The Royal Society.* Available online at: www.royalsoc.ac.uk/publication.asp?year=2005&id=2181 (accessed on 28 February 2007).

McHenry, L. B. (2006) Maxwell, Nicholas. Is science neurotic?, *Review of Metaphysics,* 59(3), p. 657(3).

McNiven, C. (2005) Review of 'Is science neurotic?' by Nicholas Maxwell, *Journal of Consciousness Studies,* 12(3), 88–89.

Midgley, M. (1986) Is wisdom forgotten?, *University Quarterly: Culture, Education and Society,* 40, 425–427.

Midgley, M. (1989) *Wisdom, information and wonder* (London, Routledge).

Muller, F. A. (2004) Maxwell's lonely war, *Studies in History and Philosophy of Modern Physics,* 35, 109–110, 117.

Newton, N. (2003) A critical review of Nicholas Maxwell's 'The human world in the physical universe', *Philosophical Psychology,* 16, 149–156.

Richards, S. (1985) Philosophical aspects of science, *Annals of Science,* 42, 348–349.

Roush, S. (2001) Review of 'The comprehensibility of the universe: a new conception of science' by Nicholas Maxwell, *The Philosophical Review,* 110, 85–87.

Schiff, M. (2005) Review of 'Is science neurotic?' by Nicholas Maxwell, *Choice,* 42(2), 2005–2006.

Schön, D. (1994) Response to: What kind of inquiry can best help us create a good world?, paper presented to the *American Association for Higher Education Conference on Faculty Roles and Rewards,* New Orleans, LA.

Shanks, N. (2000) A cosmos comprehended, *Metascience,* 9, 294–298.

Shulman, L. (1994) Response to: What kind of inquiry can best help us create a good world?, paper presented at the *American Association for Higher Education Conference on Faculty Roles and Rewards,* New Orleans, LA.

Smart, J. J. C. (2000) Review of 'The comprehensibility of the universe: a new conception of science' by Nicholas Maxwell, *British Journal for the Philosophy of Science,* 51, 907–911.

Winston, R. (2005) Who owns the science and what is the role for the scientist in future?, *Presidential Address to the British Association Festival of Science.* Available online at: www.the-ba.net/the-ba/Events/ FestivalofScience/FestivalNews/_BAPresidentialAddress2005.htm (accessed 28 February 2007).

Commercial influences on the pursuit of wisdom

Leemon B. McHenry

Commercialization of the Academy

The university of the twenty-first century has lost its way. Guided by a corporate model of research and education, it can no longer lay claim to being the guardian of truth and wisdom. This misguided state of affairs is easily traced to the 1980s when the demographic of students entering university in the US changed and educational institutions began to compete for a shrinking student population by presenting themselves as consumer-oriented (Krimsky, 2006). About the same time, legislation offered the opportunity for partnerships between academic institutions and industry, hence the appearance of the academic businessman since the 1990s pursuing grants and consultancies with profit-oriented business relations.[1] University administrations openly embraced manufacturing models of management such as 'TQM' (total quality management) and directed their faculty to approach their craft as appealing to their 'student clients'.[2] It is not at all odd to find in such institutions a carpet salesman as the university president or the salary of a football coach that far exceeds the entire budget of a humanities department.

We have entered a period in which academic leadership is no longer meaningful at the majority of educational institutions. Deans who reached their positions by virtue of distinguished contributions to their academic disciplines have been replaced with fund-raisers and academic managers, many of whom have degrees in university administration, business or educational pedagogy rather than first-order disciplines such as mathematics, biology, physics and history. This has produced a demoralizing situation in which the faculty is led by means other than the example of academic excellence.

Within this context I argue that: (1) the university has become profit driven in a way that did not exist 30 years ago; and (2) this state of affairs has worsened university-based research and the educational mission. While (1) does not seem to be in doubt since this is precisely what its chief architects had in mind, the question is whether (2) is true. Proponents of the free market economy aim to demonstrate how minimal Government regulation and the laws of supply and demand serve society best. They regard the university as a business and its students as clients or consumers of the educational prod-uct. Aside from the failure to recognize the value of education as an end in itself and the importance of critical, open inquiry to the pursuit of truth, this view has serious consequences for the common good of humanity. My goal is to focus attention on corpo-rate-sponsored research in order to show how a business-model fails to achieve anything of enduring value. While I doubt the existence of a pristine past in which universities pursued 'pure' research within an atmosphere of complete academic freedom, the current situation has taken us even further away from the ideal of free inquiry driven by the pursuit of truth.

Nicholas Maxwell has long advocated a revolution in the entire structure of academic inquiry by focusing attention on the contrast between the aims of wisdom-inquiry *vs.* knowledge-inquiry (see especially Maxwell, 1984, 2005). His work does not directly address commercialization of the academy; however, his view of a wisdom-based goal has profound implications for seeing our way clearly to the sort of free inquiry that gives wisdom rather than economic expediency the primary place in the very mission of the academy. Here I modify Maxwell's view by contrasting wisdom-inquiry with profit-inquiry. Knowledge-inquiry is the basis for profit-inquiry, since the industries that liaise with universities are knowledge based, including but not limited to biotechnology, chemistry, pharmacology, geology, computer technologies and engineering. There is, however, a critical difference between the wisdom/knowledge-inquiry and wisdom/profit-inquiry dichotomies. The human use and value of scientific knowledge lies outside the scope of knowledge-inquiry as long as genuine knowledge is acquired, whereas profit-inquiry does make such value judgments. The problem is that the motive of profit most often results in the wrong choice with regard to how the use of knowledge will enhance the overall qual-ity of life.[3] Maxwell's wisdom-inquiry raises the important issue of what exactly constitutes the right choice.

As Maxwell makes the point:

> The central task of inquiry is to devote *reason* to the enhancement of *wisdom*—wisdom being understood here as the desire, the active endeavour, and the capacity to discover and achieve what is desirable and of value in life, both for oneself and for others. (Maxwell, 1984, p. 66)

In what he calls 'rationalistic neurosis', we seem to know quite well that our goal is a more civilized world, yet our institutions are designed to do very little to achieve this goal

(Maxwell, 2005, pp. 2–4). The pursuit of knowledge as a primary goal does not address the question of what is valuable or how to achieve it. Inquiry devoted to the goal of a more civilized world would give primary focus to solving the real problems which Maxwell identifies as the development of an ecologically sustainable world in which people do not die unnecessarily for lack of food, sanitation, medical care, a world in which there is more just distribution of land, resources, and wealth among people than at present, control of population growth, solutions to urgent environmental problems, a stop to the proliferation of nuclear, chemical and biological weapons and the spread of armaments throughout the world, and the elimination of ruthless dictatorships (Maxwell, 1984, p. 67; 2005, pp. 131–132). He therefore argues that wisdom must be built into the structure of our social and political institutions so that we remain focused on the primary task of helping us solve the main problems of humanity and discover what is ultimately valuable in life (Maxwell, 1992). The point of Maxwell's work is so obvious that it has escaped notice, yet he appears to be a lone voice for wisdom in an age devoted to a piece-meal approach to knowledge and commercial profitability.

Profit-inquiry resulting from the corporate model of the university has transformed the ethos of university life and the very ideal of intellectual inquiry. Instead of making decisions about the curriculum and research based on the most important needs of humanity, the primary focus is what will result in significant revenue. There is a persistent danger that business and management studies set the model for the entire university rather than classics, philosophy, physics or biology, especially when departments are forced to show how they are profitable or how they can attract corporate sponsors and outside grant money (see especially Siegel, 2006; Andrews, 2006). One must wonder about the future of pure mathematics, symbolic logic, cosmology or Latin in a world in which business wins the day. One must wonder how this situation will produce another Bertrand Russell or Albert Einstein to inspire future generations with models of greatness.

A case of corruption in research of medicines

One place to observe the ill effects of the corporate model of the university is academic medicine. While there is little doubt that other disciplines such as physics, engineering, biology, chemistry, geology, agriculture and economics have been influenced by corporate interests in ways that do anything but promote wisdom-inquiry and solutions that aim for the betterment of humanity, the interference with medical research has demonstrated how the profit motive has produced a corruption of the very goal of medicine—'to put the life and health of [the] patient first'—which has been the professional oath of physicians beginning with Hippocrates.

Since the 1990s, one dominant theme in the medical literature is conflict of interest and the failure to disclose industry relations that bias the results of medical research (see Angell, 2000; Bekeiman *et al.*, 2003; Nature, 2001). The proliferation of connections between physicians and industry has produced an unprecedented crisis of credibility, namely, a lack of confidence in the studies that are published in the journals and in clinical medicine more generally (see Fava, 2006). Pharmaceutical companies, for example, are allowed to test their own drugs in clinical trials that are then selected for publication. In what is now well known as the 'file drawer phenomenon', the companies select the trials that show their drugs have passed a minimal test and file away the rest that have failed. Since the companies have intellectual property rights to the data that they generate, they control the dissemination of information. The result, however, is a distorted profile of the drugs that are available to prescribing physicians[4]. The companies hire contract research organizations to conduct the clinical trials, academic researchers to design the trials and act as clinical investigators, medical communication companies to ghostwrite the publications and public relations firms to promote and advertise the drugs to the public. In many cases the lead academics who are the clinical investigators in the trial and who become the 'authors' of the publications have been on the sponsor company's payroll as 'key opinion leaders' due to their influence on prescribing habits of physicians and for the prestige that their university affiliation brings to the company's products. They will also present the results of the trial at professional conferences and promote the drugs in continuing medical education lectures. When the drugs face product liability suits in the courts, these same individuals will serve as expert witnesses in defense of the manufacturer.

Thus far this situation may not seem altogether different from the sort of relationship academics have with the publishing industry in that they will engage in a consultancy with one or more companies and join the advisory board as experts in the field, but this analogy neglects the most egregious problems of the corruption of research by manipulation of scientific results and a distortion of research priorities. There is also a significant difference between a consulting arrangement in which an academic provides an independent evaluation of the quality of a book or a series and one in which an academic promotes a product and in many cases owns stock in the company that produces it. The drug companies do not retain key opinion leaders for the acute, critical evaluation of their drugs.

Since the companies invest enormous sums to bring new drugs onto the market, failure is not an option. Aside from suppression of data in publication results, the very design of the trial is often manipulated in subtle ways that escape detection in the peer-review process. Conducting the trial drug against a treatment known to be inferior, testing it against too low a dose of the competitor drug, excluding placebo responders in the wash out phase of the trial, or using multiple endpoints in the protocol in order to select for publication the ones that produce favorable results are all common strategies of ensuring success (see Smith, 2005). When it comes to writing up the results, the sponsor company's marketing department contracts with the public relations firm and the medical writers to produce the manuscript. This typically involves several drafts of the article that are then inspected by the academic 'authors' and the sponsor company's marketing and legal departments for approval. The marketing department in connection with the public relations firm or the medical communication firm will also select the target journal well in advance of the trial results, respond to criticism from the peer-review process and in letters to the editor post-publication, and organize the distribution of journal reprints to the pharmaceutical sales force. When the article appears in the target journal, the ghostwriter either disappears or is acknowledged in the fine print as having provided 'editorial assistance'. The job of the ghost, after all, is to remain invisible in order to conceal conflicts of interest with industry and create the appearance of objective science. In some of the worst instances, the academic co-conspirators in this process are simply paid to have their names appear on papers in which they played no role at all (see Fugh-Berman, 2005; McHenry, 2005; Kassirer, 2005). In this manner, the much esteemed peer-review process has devolved into an information-laundering operation for the pharmaceutical companies (Horton, 2004). Medical journal articles reporting on drug trials have become little more than advertisements (Healy, 2004b).

While some of the editors of the leading medical journals have fought to expose the degree to which their literature has been infiltrated by industry, there is enormous pressure on editors to adopt positions that favor the companies (Horton, 2004, p. 7; also see Lexchin & Light, 2006). The publishers or scientific societies that own the medical journals derive enormous revenue from the pharmaceutical advertising and the commercially valuable content which nets the journal handsome sums in the sale of re-prints (Smith, 2006; Glassman et al 1999). Universities that profit from the clinical trial revenue also play a part in maintaining this situation since there is little motivation to investigate their own academics for scientific misconduct or for inflating their CVs with the ghostwritten publications. For one of many such conflicts of interest, see Bass (1999). How this behavior serves as a model for students who might feel the pressure to cut corners or fudge research results is disturbing, especially in a field in which the consequences are potentially fatal.

We all become guinea pigs in post-marketing surveillance given the failure to convey honestly the results of research that brings the drugs to market. The stories of the painkiller, rofecoxib (Vioxx), and the anti-depressants such as paroxetine (Paxil, Seroxat) have been exposed in the lay press, but they are merely two examples of the general problem with corporate-sponsored research and a failure of Government to regulate (see Kesselheim & Avron, 2007). It would seem that rigorous testing of their drugs would be in the company's best, long-term interest, but as long as the corporate structure is led by marketing rather than science there is very little that will alter the goal of maximizing the value of their shareholder's stock. Even the probability of expensive litigation is calculated into the cost-benefit analysis of bringing a new drug on the market.

Another major issue of concern in medicine related to the influence of the pharmaceutical industry is marketing strategies designed to increase artificially the number of patients on their drugs. This occurs in a number of ways: first involving the creation of patient support groups and patient compliance programmes, both of which are fronts for the companies; second in the way that the companies liaise with medical organizations in defining diseases or treatment; and third in the attempt to gain regulatory approval or promote off-label use for many indications of the same medicine.

Pharmaceutical companies operate behind the scenes by sponsoring support groups and compliance programs to make sure as many people as possible become consumers of their products and remain on these products for as long as possible. Since the companies realize that the doctors are crucial to expanding these markets, development of key opinion leaders serves the goals of creating awareness of the dangers of undiagnosed 'disease' and introducing the drugs into as many hospital formularies as possible. What appears to be in the best interest of patients, however, is in reality a marketing strategy designed to convince people that something is wrong with them that requires pharmacotherapy. A recent UK House of Commons report on the influence of the pharmaceutical industry identifies this phenomenon as 'the medicalization of society', namely, the 'trend towards categorizing more and more individuals as "abnormal" or in need of drug treatment' when in fact the so-called diseases requiring treatment are merely ordinary conditions of life (House of Commons Health Committee, 2005, pp. 100–101). When does worry become 'general anxiety disorder' or shyness become 'social anxiety disorder'? When is inability to concentrate 'attention deficit disorder' or premenstrual syndrome 'premenstrual dysphoric disorder'? While there is an important question in medicine about whether and when patients should be on medications to treat high blood pressure or high cholesterol, in psychiatry the categories of illness multiply with each appearance of a new edition of the *Diagnostic and statistical manual of mental disorders* (DSM) (American Psychiatric Association, 2005). The committees formed to provide the definitions in this bible of psychiatry are composed of psychiatrists who have extensive ties to industry, including key opinion leaders. This has led to the charge of 'disease mongering' in a profession that is almost entirely dependent on the pharmaceutical industry (see Moynihan & Cassels, 2005; McHenry, 2006).

Once a drug is tested in clinical trials and gains regulatory approval it is licensed for an 'indication', major depressive disorder, for example. But the company might also test the same drug for social anxiety disorder, pedophilia or compulsive shopping. In the parlance of industry this is known as 'evergreening'. In order to develop 'green' pastures for potential markets, regulatory approval of several indications means more patients taking the same drug. One investigation into the process of approval showed in the case of antidepressants the standard 'better than nothing' means a clinically negligible advantage of the drug over placebo. In some studies, placebo control groups duplicated 80% of the response to medication (see Smith, 2000; Krisch *et al.*, 2002). Even when the drugs are not approved, they can still be prescribed 'off-label', if the prescribing physician believes the drug will benefit the patient. While it is illegal for the companies to promote their drugs off-label, key opinion leaders will engage in their promotional efforts for them by presenting the results of the trials at scientific conferences and signing on to the ghostwritten articles that claim the drugs are safe and effective.

Finally, instead of focusing attention on the greater medical needs of the world's population, the profit motive of pharmaceutical research gives priority to the development of blockbuster drugs that are promoted and sold to the wealthy first-world countries (Chirac & Torreele, 2006). Here again the markets are created and expanded by advertising campaigns and promotional efforts described above. The drive is to develop similar chemical compounds that are already manufactured by competing companies for what, in many cases, are relatively trivial conditions or lifestyle problems. So, for example drugs that treat heartburn, obesity, hair loss, toenail fungus, sexual performance, depression, allergies, high cholesterol, and the like will provide enormous profits to the companies while other important drugs that are less profitable will not be developed or will be discontinued. Examples of this latter group include certain anesthetics, antivenins, antidotes for drug overdoses, anticlotting drugs, antibiotics, and vaccines against flu and pneumonia, many of which are lifesaving treatments (Angell, 2004, pp. 91–93). While newly-developed drugs to treat HIV/ AIDS might be thought of as a counter-example to the view argued for here, a deeper investigation of such advances reveals that the real source of success was not profit-inquiry via key opinion leader development, but rather liaisons between government, universities and other non-profit research before the compounds were handed over to private drug companies for further development, manufacture and distribution (see Angell, 2004; National Institutes of Health, 2000; Consumer Project on Technology, 2000).

In summary then the general complaint heard in both the mainstream medical journals and in the urgent need to warn the public in the lay media is that marketing has usurped science as the results of rigged clinical trials have infiltrated the peer-reviewed literature and disinformed physicians about the true risks and benefits of medication (in addition to Angell, Kassirer, Healy, and Moynihan and Cassels above, see Avorn, 2004; Law, 2006). Academics have compromised the integrity of their fields by becoming a party to scientific fraud and the attempt of industry to gain complete control of medicine by manufacturing consensus. Message-driven models of public relations strategy have become the standard against data-driven science due to the simple fact that industry is the funding source. This is a serious problem in what is meant to be an age of evidence-based medicine. Moreover, there is the central problem concerning the manner in which commercial pressures distort priorities of research, which in the case of developing medicines results in choices driven by maximizing profit rather than greater medical needs. In both of these aspects— scientific testing and establishing priorities—we see how profit-inquiry fails to produce anything of lasting value for humanity. What value there is at present is largely the result of breakthroughs made decades ago. As David Healy makes the point: 'We are living off scientific capital accumulated in an earlier age' (Healy, 2006, p. 17).

The focus of my case against the corruption of medicine is industry-sponsored clinical research, the involvement of academics in lending credibility to biased testing, and promotion masquerading as science. This malpractice should not, however, be understood to apply to the whole of medicine, including practising doctors and nurses who adhere to their professional duties with utmost concern for principles of altruism.

The relevance of Popper's critical rationalism

In a world in which medicine is sponsored by GlaxoSmithKline, Eli Lilly, Pfizer and Merck, geology by Exxon, British Petroleum, and Chevron, nutrition by the McDonalds Corporation and Kraft Foods, and physics by Rockwell Aerospace and General Electric, the common good of humanity is replaced by competition of special interests, all of which are engaged in marketing and promotion rather than a critical assessment of ideas. How far one can extrapolate from the example of academic medicine is unclear. Some relations between industry and the academy will have less corruptive effects. As Arthur Schafer points to the negative effects of commercialization on biomedical and fossil fuel energy research, he argues:

> The fundamental ethos of contemporary scientific research has evolved so rapidly during the past few decades that it would scarcely count as hyperbole were one to describe the process as a 'revolution,' or perhaps as a 'commercial revolution'.... Although no branch of inquiry, from agriculture to climate change, has escaped the revolution, the change has been more dramatic in the field of biomedicine than in any other area of university research. (Schafer, 2004, p.14)[5]

The broad consequence of this situation, which I believe is very close to what we have at present, is that our ideal of an open, democratic society is threatened by an oligarchy of corporations. I argue that the university must assume the responsibility of the common good of humanity and the pursuit of truth above and beyond special corporate interests. Instead, universities deprived of proper funding from Government have become instruments of industry by doing their research for them or serving as agents for the promotion of their products.

In this context, I suggest that a combination of Karl Popper's critical rationalism and Maxwell's philosophy of wisdom would restore the integrity of the university. In place of the propaganda model, which Popper viewed as an integral part of the closed, totalitarian society, he argued that true intellectual advance depends on rigorous criticism, first in the genuine testing of scientific hypotheses and second in the assessment of ideas more generally. The freedom to advance ideas and have them properly tested is the basis of our cherished open, democratic society (Popper, 1945). But it appears that we merely pay lip service to the ideal of democracy when corporate interests dominate aspects of our society where they do not belong.

For Popper it is always easy to get confirmations of scientific hypotheses—especially, I would add, when industry is in control of the process—but a genuine test must risk falsifying the theory being tested. Protecting the hypotheses by ad hoc modifications or by designing experiments that make them immune from refutation always lowers the scientific status of the views advanced or puts them into the same category as pseudo-science (Popper, 1963). As a methodology of science, Popper's falsificationist theory has been embraced as the most accurate description of the aims of rigorous science. Applying Popper's ideas to the case of industry-sponsored research of medicines, when knowledge is viewed as the intellectual property of the industry that has sponsored the research, we have nothing but the marketplace itself as the test. Yet the current state of medicine has shown the marketplace has generally failed to expose the extent of the corruption, or to reveal the flaws in products fast enough to protect patients from serious harm and death. Industry is not programmed to do the critical, scientific testing; rather it is designed to circumvent the process to minimize financial loss, eliminate competition and suppress criticism.

Popper would have certainly viewed the activities of the pharmaceutical industry as a decisive step backwards, as a sort of promotional ideology rather than a serious science, and as a failure of Government to protect science from those political forces that favor the interests of industry. In *The poverty of historicism*, he imagines conditions under which scientific progress would be arrested, and with uncanny vision into our current situation, he discusses the control of laboratories for research, suppression of control of scientific periodicals, and the suppression or control of scientific conferences and universities. Science cannot advance when certain theories, hypotheses and views are protected, and especially when the testing itself is manipulated such that falsification is impossible. Popper recognized ultimately that 'progress depends very largely on political factors; on political institutions that safeguard the freedom of thought: on democracy' (Popper, 1961, p. 155). The free market cannot trump the interest of the open society in scientific progress.

When Popper generalized his falsificationist conception of scientific method to social and political problems in his critical rationalism, it became clear that he had foremost in mind the benefits of intellectual honesty and some form of rational testing for a liberal democracy. Truth does not come easy. The proper job of the university is to guard against facile, superficial, or commercialized conceptions of the good life. Indoctrination in ideology and promotional models of business are not education. But Popper's critical rationalism does not quite take us far enough to the pursuit of wisdom. His focus was the objectivity of knowledge and as such he embraced a form of what Maxwell called 'knowledge-inquiry' or the 'philosophy of knowledge' by construing social problems as problems of the social sciences aimed at the discovery of scientific social laws. As Maxwell writes:

> Popper's line of argument has the effect of prohibiting the one social change that is now so urgently needed if humanity is to discover, little by little, how to tackle its common problems in more cooperative and humane ways—namely a change in academic inquiry, and above all in social inquiry, from knowledge to wisdom ...

> According to the philosophy of wisdom, it is the fundamental intellectual obligation of every teacher, every social inquirer, every scientist and scholar, in his or her professional work, to put forward and criticize proposals for cooperative action intended to promote the realization of what is of value in life and to encourage others to do this. ... The vital point is to promote in a society the *habit* of putting forward and criticizing proposals for action intended to help achieve what is of value. (Maxwell, 1984, pp. 196–197)

While the proponents of knowledge-inquiry such as Popper have a legitimate complaint against the manipulation of scientific results, profit-inquiry remains silent. Where the flaws are most obviously revealed in knowledge-inquiry, however, is with respect to assigning priorities to research, for here there is nothing that directs us to promoting human welfare or working for the relief of avoidable suffering. Maxwell's wisdom-inquiry addresses both problems of corruption of the scientific process by commercial influences and the misaligned goals of research that result from profit-inquiry.

Conclusion

Socrates is the anti-corporate hero in commercially prosperous but wisdom impoverished Athens in the fifth century BC. He devoted his life to the achievement of wisdom and exhorted his fellow citizens to pursue what is of ultimate value in life rather than material pleasures and the pursuit of moneymaking. This became one essential part of Plato's vision of the ideal state in his *Republic*. Plato saw quite clearly that the guardians of wisdom had to be protected from commercial influence. They were therefore selected for their intellectual vigor rather than their appetite for property (Plato, *The Republic*, chapters 10 and 11). Western democracies have failed to take notice of the relevance of this mechanism for preventing corruption in our political leadership. Popper famously rejected Plato's idea of the philosopher-kings as a totalitarian betrayal of Socrates since the morals of the *polis* were to be protected by a strict censorship and the commands of the philosopher-kings enforced by a special class of guardians (Popper, 1945). However, there is most certainly agreement here about the need to protect intellectual inquiry from the special interests of industry. The university must guard against becoming an extension of these interests. What we gain in long-term service to humanity is far greater than what we lose in monetary embellishment of the institution.

Acknowledgements

I wish to thank Nicholas Maxwell, Joel Lexchin, David Barry, George Allan and an anonymous peer reviewer for constructive criticism to earlier drafts of this paper.

Notes

1. The Bayh-Dole Act or Patent and Trademark Law Amendments Act of 1980 for example gave US universities intellectual property control of their inventions that resulted from federal Government-funded research. For a discussion of the effects of Bayh-Dole and the privatization of knowledge, see Horton (2004).
2. While I write from the point of view of an academic in the US, my impression is that universities in the UK are on a similar path even if the details of the emergence differ. Six books that address the erosion of scholarly independence in the market model university and the threat to the future of intellectual inquiry in North America include: Lawrence C. Soley, *Leasing the ivory tower: the corporate takeover of academia* (1995), Sheila Slaughter and Larry L. Leslie, *Academic capitalism: politics, policies and the entrepreneurial university* (1997), Neil Tudiver, *Universities for sale: resisting corporate control over Canadian higher education* (1999), Geoffrey D. White and Flannery C. Hauck (Eds) *Campus, Inc. corporate power in the ivory tower* (2000), Derek Bok, *Universities in the marketplace: the commercialization of higher education* (2004) and Sheldon Krimsky, *Science in the private interest: has the lure of profits corrupted biomedical research?* (2003).
3. Whereas Maxwell's focus is the quality of human life, I should include both human and non-human animals in the calculus. I assume here that Maxwell would object to the knowledge resulting from vivisection or other painful experiments on non-human animals even if this knowledge were to benefit humans.
4. The cases of David Healy, Nancy Olivieri and Aubrey Blumsohn have shown the consequences to medical careers for those who refuse to read the results of research in the manner prescribed by the sponsor companies. For Healy, see his *Let Them Eat Prozac* (2004a); for the case of Olivieri, see Schafer (2007, pp. 111-115); for the case of Blumsohn, see Baty (2005, p. 9). Schafer explicitly connects the biomedical scandals of Healy and Olivieri with corporate sponsorship of research in his 'Biomedical conflicts of interest: a defense of the sequestration thesis—learning from the cases of Nancy Olivieri and David Healy' (2004, pp. 8-24).
5. Aside from biomedical research, Schafer points to the British government's 'subsidizing the oil and gas industry's profits to the tune of 40 million pounds every year through the "capture" of some of Britain's most respected academic institutions'.

Notes on contributor

Leemon McHenry is lecturer in philosophy at California State University, Northridge. His research interests include metaphysics, philosophy of science and medical ethics.

References

American Psychiatric Association (2005) *Diagnostic and statistical manual of mental disorders* (Washington, DC, American Psychiatric Association).
Andrews, J. G. (2006) How we can resist corporatization, *Academe: Bulletin of the American Association of University Professors,* May/June, 16–19.
Angell, M. (2000) Is academic medicine for sale?, *The New England Journal of Medicine,* 342, 1516–1518.
Angell, M. (2004) *The truth about the drug companies: how they deceive us and what to do about it* (New York, Random House).

Avorn, J. (2004) *Powerful medicines: the benefits, risks, and costs of prescriptions drugs* (New York, Alfred A. Knoff).

Bass, A. (1999, October 4) Drug companies enrich Brown Professor, *Boston Globe*, p. A01. Available online at: www.narpa.org/drug_companies_enrich_researcher.htm (accessed March 2007).

Baty, P. (2005, November 25) Data row sparks research debate, *Times Higher Education Supplement*, p. 9.

Bekeiman, J. E., Li, Y. & Gross, C. P. (2003) Scope and impact of financial conflicts of interest in biomedical research, *Journal of the American Medical Association*, 289, 454–465.

Bok, D. (2004) *Universities in the marketplace: the commercialization of higher education* (Princeton, Princeton University Press).

Chirac, P. & Torreele, E. (2006) Global framework on essential health R&D, *Lancet*, 367, 1560–1561.

Consumer Project on Technology (2000) *Additional notes of government role in the development of HIV/AIDS drugs.* Available online at: www.cptech.org/ip/health/aids/gov-role.html (accessed March 2007).

Fava, G. A. (2006) A different medicine is possible, *Psychotherapy and Psychosomatics*, 75, 1–3.

Fugh-Berman, A. (2005) The corporate coauthor, *Journal of General Internal Medicine*, 20, 546–548.

Glassman, P. A., Hunter-Hayes, J. & Nakamura, T. (1999) Pharmaceutical advertising revenue and physicians organizations: how much is too much?, *Western Journal of Medicine*, 171, 234–238.

Healy, D. (2004a) *Let them eat prozac: the unhealthy relationship between the pharmaceutical industry and depression* (New York, New York University Press).

Healy, D. (2004b) Manufacturing consensus, *Hastings Center Report*, 34, inside back cover.

Healy, D. (2006, August 18) Hasty bolt down the aisle or a well-considered union?, *The Times Higher Educational Supplement*, pp. 16–17.

Horton, R. (2004) The dawn of McScience, *The New York Review of Books*, 51, 7–9.

House of Commons Health Committee (2005) *The influence of the pharmaceutical industry.* Volume 1 (London, The Stationery Office).

Kassirer, J. P. (2005) *On the take: how America's complicity with big business can endanger your health* (New York, Oxford University Press).

Kesselheim, A. S. & Avorn, J. (2007) The role of litigation in defining drug risks, *Journal of the American Medical Association*, 297, 308–311.

Krimsky, S. (2003) *Science in the private interest: has the lure of profits corrupted biomedical research?* (Lanham, MD, Rowman and Littlefield).

Krimsky, S. (2006) Autonomy, disinterest, and entrepreneurial science, *Society*, 43(4), 22–29.

Krisch, I., Moore, T. J., Scoboria, A. & Nicholls, S. S. (2002) The Emperor's new drugs: an analysis of antidepressant medication data submitted to the US food and drug administration, *Prevention and Treatment*, 5(23). Available online at: www.alphastim.com/Information/Technology/Research/Research_PDF/EmperorsNewDrugs.pdf (accessed March 2007).

Law, J. (2006) *Big pharma: exposing the global healthcare agenda* (New York, Carroll and Graf Publishers).

Lexchin, J. & Light, D. W. (2006) Commercial influence and the content of medical journals, *British Medical Journal*, 332, 1444–1447.

Maxwell, N. (1984) *From knowledge to wisdom* (Oxford, Blackwell).

Maxwell, N. (1992) What kind of inquiry can best help us create a good world?, *Science, Technology, and Human Values*, 17(2), 205–227.

Maxwell, N. (2005) *Is science neurotic?* (London, Imperial College Press).

McHenry, L. (2005) On the origin of great ideas: science in the age of big pharma, *Hastings Center Report*, 35, 17–19.

McHenry, L. (2006) Ethical issues in psychopharmacology, *Journal of Medical Ethics*, 32, 405–410.

Moynihan, R. & Cassels, A. (2005) *Selling sickness: how the world's biggest pharmaceutical companies are turning us all into patients* (New York, Nation Books).

National Institutes of Health (2000) *NIH contributions to pharmaceutical development: case study analysis of the top-selling drugs* (Bethesda, MD, Office of Science Policy).

Nature, (2001) Is the university-industrial complex out of control, *Nature*, 409(6817), 119.

Plato, *Republic*, volume 1 (B. Jowett, Trans., 1937) (New York, Random House).

Popper, K. (1945) *The open society and its enemies.* 2 volumes (London, Routledge).

Popper, K. (1961) *The poverty of historicism* (New York, Torchbooks).

Popper, K. (1963) *Conjectures and refutations: the growth of scientific knowledge* (London, Routledge).

Schafer, A. (2004) Biomedical conflicts of interest: a defense of the sequestration thesis—learning from the cases of Nancy Olivieri and David Healy, *Journal of Medical Ethics*, 30, 8–24.

Schafer, A. (2007) Commentary: science scandal or ethics scandal? Olivieri redux, *Bioethics*, 21(2), 111–115.

Siegel, D. J. (2006) Minding the academy's business, *Academe: Bulletin of the American Association of University Professors*, November/December, 55–57.

Slaughter, S. & Leslie, L. L. (1997) *Academic capitalism: politics, policies and the entrepreneurial university* (Baltimore, Johns Hopkins University Press).

Smith, D. C. (2000) Antidepressant efficacy, *Ethical Human Sciences and Services*, 2/3, 215–216.

Smith, R. (2005) Medical journals are an extension of the marketing arm of pharmaceutical companies, *Plos Medicine*, 2, e138. Available online at: http://medicine.plosjournals.org (accessed September 2006).

Smith, R. (2006) Lapses at the New England Journal of Medicine, *Journal of the Royal Society of Medicine*, 99, 1–3.

Soley, L. C. (1995) *Leasing the ivory tower: the corporate takeover of academia* (Boston, South End Press).

Tudiver, N. (1999) *Universities for sale: resisting corporate control over Canadian higher education* (Toronto, James Lorimer).

White, G. D. & C. Hauck, F. C. (Eds) (2000) *Campus, Inc. corporate power in the ivory tower* (Amherst, Prometheus Books).

Teaching for wisdom: what matters is not just what students know, but how they use it

Robert J. Sternberg, Alina Reznitskaya and Linda Jarvin

Introduction

A few years ago, one of us was on his way to an important meeting but got stuck in a maddening traffic jam. As he approached an exit along our slow, bumpy and obstacle-laden route, he observed that the highway that extended out from the exit, which was perpendicular to the direction in which he was going, was wonderfully paved and the traffic was moving rapidly with no obstacles along its course. He considered taking that route. There was only one problem: the route led nowhere he wanted or needed to go, nor that he should have gone. Nevertheless, it was just so tempting. After all, the route led somewhere! Since then, many times when he has been in horribly long lines for flights to his destination, or has seen one flight after another to that destination cancelled, he has been tempted to go somewhere else where it is easier and quicker to go.

Education has taken the easier, quicker route. It leads students rapidly and relatively smoothly—in the wrong direction. That wrong direction is illustrated by the high-stakes systems of testing that have come to dominate the UK as well as the US. It is not that high-stakes testing is, in itself, necessarily bad. It is that what the tests measure, to a large extent, doesn't matter all that much in the long run. What matters is not *only* how much knowledge you have, but how you use that knowledge—whether for good ends (as for Mahatma Gandhi or Martin Luther King) or for bad ones (as for Adolf Hitler and Joseph Stalin). In this article, we argue that what matters most of all is the development of wisdom.

The purpose of education is to develop not only knowledge and skills, but the ability to use one's knowledge and skills effectively. Many societies today are preoccupied with the development of knowledge and basic cognitive skills in school children. But are knowledge and basic cognitive skills—the essential ingredients of intelligence as classically defined (see Herrnstein & Murray, 1994)—enough? Consider the following.

Flynn (1998) has pointed out that in more than a dozen countries for which records have been available, IQs have been rising roughly at a rate of 9 points per generation (30 years). This increase has been going on for at least several generations (see also Neisser, 1998).

With IQs going up and IQ-related abilities counting more and more for success in the society, one can only conclude that the IQ-like abilities of those at the top of the socio-economic spectrum are higher than ever before—even higher than would be predicted merely by the 'Flynn effect', because IQs have become more important for gaining access to higher education and premium jobs. But again, the rise in IQs among the socioeconomic elite does not seem to have created a happier or more harmonious society, and one only has to read the daily newspapers to see examples of the poor uses to which high IQ can be put. Judging by the amount, seriousness, and sheer scale of global conflict, perhaps not much of the increase in IQ is going towards creating a common good. Certainly there is no reason to believe that increasing IQs have improved people's or nations' relations with each other. Indeed, today there is more terrorism than at any time in recent memory. In the 1990s, there were more genocides and massacres than at any time since the Second World War. As people became smarter, they became, if anything, less wise and moved further from—rather than closer to—the pursuit of a common good. Indeed, there seems to be a great deal of hate in today's world (Sternberg, 2003).

The memory and analytical skills that are so central to intelligence are certainly important for school and life success, but perhaps they are not sufficient. For one thing, there is more to intelligence than just these skills (Gardner, 1983; Sternberg, 1997). For another thing, one can be smart but foolish. We have seen this in political leaders and in business leaders, such as at Enron, Arthur Andersen, WorldCom, and elsewhere. Smart but foolish people are susceptible to one or more of six fallacies (Sternberg, 2002), which we will illustrate with the use of Enron:

- *Unrealistic optimism.* They believe they are so smart that whatever they do will work out just fine, regardless of whether it really makes sense. Top-level executives at Enron believed they could create shell companies to hide losses and that all then would be all right.

- *Egocentrism.* They start to view decisions only in terms of how the decisions benefit them. Top Enron managers enriched themselves at the expense of shareholders, employees, customers and other stakeholders.
- *Omniscience.* They think they are all-knowing; they don't know what they don't know. Top Enron managers believed they knew how to run a company, and as a result, failed to learn from mistakes.
- *Omnipotence.* They think they can do whatever they want. Top Enron managers engaged in accounting fraud, even though they knew it was illegal.
- *Invulnerability.* They think they are so smart they can get away with anything they do. The top Enron managers thought they could get away with insider trading and misleading the public.
- *Ethical disengagement.* They tend to ignore the ethical dimension of the problems they face, believing themselves to be above such matters. They view ethics as important— but for other people. Top Enron managers ignored ethical principles in the way they ran their business.

Students and teachers alike can realize that fallacies such as these are not just mistakes 'other people' make. We all are susceptible to foolish thinking. Indeed, the 'smarter' we are, the more we may think ourselves immune. And it is this fantasy that we are immune that makes us all the more susceptible. Arguably, wisdom is at least as important as, or even more important than, sheer knowledge and intelligence. Thus, promoting the development of wisdom in schools represents a clear need and responsibility.

What is wisdom?

Wisdom can be defined as the 'power of judging rightly and following the soundest course of action, based on knowledge, experience, understanding, etc' (*Webster's new world dictionary*, 1997, p. 1533). A number of psychologists have attempted to understand wisdom in more variegated ways. The approaches underlying some of these attempts are summarized in Baltes and Staudinger (in press), Sternberg (1990, 1998a), and Sternberg and Jordan (2005). It is beyond the scope of this article to review all these different approaches.

Wisdom is defined here as the application of intelligence, creativity, and knowledge as mediated by values toward the achievement of a common good through a *balance* among (a) intrapersonal, (b) interpersonal, and (c) extrapersonal interests, over the (a) short- and (b) long-terms, in order to achieve a balance among (a) adaptation to existing environments, (b) shaping of existing environments, and (c) selection of new environments (Sternberg, 1998a, 2001), as shown in Figure 1. We make no claim that ours is the only definition of wisdom (see Sternberg & Jordan, 2005) or even the 'best' one. It is, however, a definition we have found to be useful in designing a program for developing wisdom in young students.

Thus, wisdom is not just about maximizing one's own or someone else's self-interest, but also about balancing off various self-interests (intrapersonal) with the interests of others (interpersonal) and of other aspects of the context in which one lives (extrapersonal), such as one's city or country or environment or religion.

Goal   **Common Good**

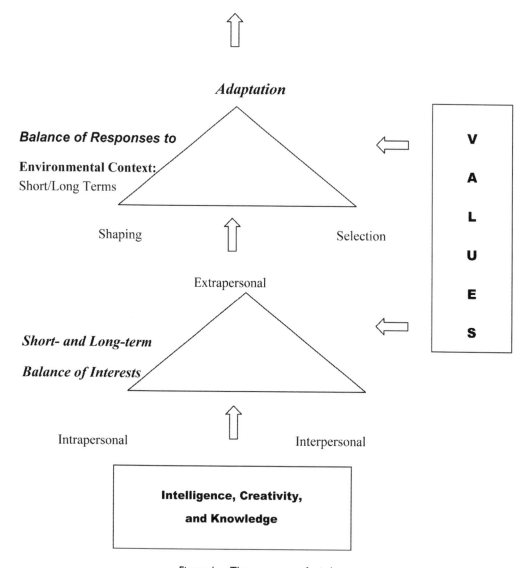

Figure 1.   The structure of wisdom

An implication of this view is that when one applies intelligence, creativity and knowledge, one may seek deliberately outcomes that are good for oneself and bad for others. In wisdom, however, one certainly may seek good ends for oneself, but one also seeks good outcomes for others. If one's motivations are to maximize certain people's interests and minimize other people's, wisdom is not involved. In wisdom, one seeks a common good, realizing that this common good may be better for some than for others.

We refer here to 'interests', which are related to the multiple points of view that are a common feature of many theories of wisdom (as reviewed in Sternberg, 1990). Diverse interests encompass multiple points of view, and thus the use of the term 'interests' is intended to include 'points of view'. Sometimes differences in points of view derive not so much from differences in cognitions as from differences in motivations, as when teachers and boards of education have different ideas about how scarce budget dollars should be spent.

Problems requiring wisdom always involve at least some element of each of intrapersonal, interpersonal, and extrapersonal interests. For example, one might decide that it is wise to take a particular teaching position, a decision that seemingly involves only one person. But many people are typically affected by an individual's decision to take a job—significant others, children, perhaps parents and friends. In addition, one might consider extrapersonal and long-term interests, such as the societal needs to contribute to the education of new immigrants in urban settings. And the decision always has to be made in the context of the whole range of available options. Similarly, a decision about whether to increase the importance of high-stakes testing requires wisdom because it involves the people who take the tests, their parents, their school, and the society. Wisdom involves a balancing not only of the three kinds of interests, but also of three possible courses of action in response to this balancing: adaptation of oneself or others to existing environments; shaping of environments in order to render them more compatible with oneself or others; and selection of new environments (Sternberg, 1985, 1997). In adaptation, the individual tries to find ways to conform to the existing environment that forms his or her context. Sometimes, adaptation is the best course of action under a given set of circumstances. But typically one seeks a balance between adaptation and shaping, realizing that fit to an environment requires not only changing oneself, but changing the environment as well. When an individual finds it impossible or at least implausible to attain such a fit, he or she may decide to select a new environment altogether, leaving, for example, a job, a community, a marriage, or whatever.

Wise thinking will not develop simply by teaching for other kinds of thinking. It needs to be targeted directly. How might it be nurtured? *And why is it so scarce?*

Implications for education

Increases in intelligence—at least as measured by IQ—have not been matched by obvious comparable increases in wisdom. Indeed, to the extent that our society has increasingly stressed the use of IQ to maximize one's own chances of admission to and success in the 'cognitive elite' posited by Herrnstein and Murray (1994), increases in IQ may have been concomitant with decreases in wisdom. High IQ with a scarcity of wisdom has brought us a world with the power to finish itself off many times over.

Wisdom might bring us a world that would seek instead to better itself and the conditions of all the people in it. At some level, we as a society have a choice. What do we wish to maximize through our schooling? Is it only knowledge? Is it only intelligence? Or is it knowledge, intelligence, and wisdom too? If it is wisdom too, then we can put our students on a much different course. We can value not only how students use their individual abilities to maximize their own attainments but how they use these abilities to maximize the attainments of others as well. We can, in short, value wisdom.

What would an education look like that valued wisdom? Consider the principles we are using to promote the development of wisdom in middle-school students in the US public schools. In our newly designed curriculum, we infused wisdom-related instruction into the teaching of American history.

Principles of teaching for wisdom derived from the balance theory of wisdom

Teachers who teach for wisdom will explore with students the notion that conventional abilities and achievements are not enough for a satisfying life. Many people become trapped in their lives and, despite feeling conventionally successful, feel that their lives lack fulfillment. Fulfillment is not an alternative to success, but rather, is an aspect of it that, for most people, goes beyond money, promotions, large houses, and so forth. The teacher will further demonstrate and encourage students to consider how wisdom is critical for a satisfying life. In the long run, wise decisions benefit people in ways that foolish decisions never do. The teacher can teach students the usefulness of interdependence—a rising tide raises all ships; a falling tide can sink them.

It is also useful to role model wisdom, because what you do is more important than what you say. Typical school matters, ranging from classroom discipline issues to student elections, could offer teachers and students multiple opportunities to demonstrate and practise wisdom. By helping students learn to properly balance competing interests and goals involved in much of everyday decision-making, teachers can instill new, more caring ways of participating in a school community. Teachers can help students recognize their own interests, those of other people, and those of institutions. They will teach students that the 'means' by which the end is obtained matters, not just the end.

Students can be encouraged to form, critique, and integrate their own values in their thinking. They can read about wise judgments and decision making in the context of the actions that followed so that the students understand that such means of judging and decision making exist. They further can learn to think dialectically (Hegel, 1931), realizing that both questions and their answers evolve over time, and that the answer to an important life question can differ at different times in one's life (such as whether to marry). Wisdom further requires students to learn to think dialogically, whereby they understand interests and ideas from multiple points of view. For example, what one group views as a 'settler', another may view as an 'invader'. Most importantly, students can learn to search for and then try to reach the common good—a good where everyone wins and not only those with whom one identifies.

Teaching for wisdom will succeed only if teachers encourage and reward wisdom. Teachers can make wisdom real for students' lives. Teachers can teach students to monitor events in their lives and their own thought processes about these events. One way to learn to recognize others' interests is to begin to identify your own. They also can help students understand the importance of inoculating oneself against the pressures of unbalanced self-interests and small-group interests.

Students will develop wisdom by becoming engaged in class discussions, projects, and essays that encourage them to discuss the lessons they have learned from both classical and modern works and how these lessons can be applied to their own lives and the lives of others. They can study not only 'truth', as we know it, but values. The idea is not to force-feed a set of values, but to encourage students reflectively to develop their own prosocial ones.

Students can be encouraged to think about how almost everything they study might be used for better or worse ends, and to realize that the ends to which knowledge is put *do* matter. Teachers can realize that the only way they can develop wisdom in their students is to serve as role models of wisdom themselves. A role model of wisdom will take a much more Socratic approach to teaching than teachers customarily do. Students often want large quantities of information spoon-fed or even force-fed to them. They then attempt to memorize this material for exams, only to forget it soon thereafter. In a wisdom-based approach to teaching, students will need to take a more active role in constructing their learning. But a wisdom-based approach is not, in my view, tantamount to a constructivist approach to learning. Students have not achieved or even come close to achieving wisdom when they merely have constructed their own learning. Rather, they must be able to construct knowledge not only from their own point of view, but also to construct and sometimes reconstruct knowledge from the point of view of others. Constructivism from only a single point of view can lead to egocentric rather than balanced understanding.

Lessons taught to emphasize wisdom would have a rather different character from lessons as they are often taught today. Consider examples.

First, social studies and especially history lessons would look very different. For example, high school American history books typically teach American history from only one point of view, that of the new Americans. Thus Columbus is referred to as having 'discovered' America, a strange notion from the standpoint of the many occupants who already lived there when it was 'discovered'. The conquest of the southwest and the Alamo also are presented only from the point of view of the new settlers, not from the standpoint of, say, the Mexicans who lost roughly half their territory. This kind of ethnocentric and frankly propagandistic teaching would have no place in a curriculum that sought to develop wisdom and an appreciation of the need to balance interests.

Second, science teaching would not be about facts presented as though they are the final word. Science is often taught as though it represents the end point of a process of evolution of thought rather than one of many midpoints (Sternberg, 1998b). Students could scarcely realize from this kind of teaching that the paradigms of today, and thus the theories and findings that emanate from them, will eventually be superseded, much as the paradigms, theories, and findings of yesterday were replaced by those of today. Students further can learn that, contrary to the way many textbooks are written, the classical 'scientific method' is largely a particular approach rather than a fixed set of processes and that scientists are as susceptible to fads as are members of other groups. In other words, it is important that students interact critically with information presented in science textbooks.

Third, teaching of literature can reflect a kind of balance that is often absent. The study of literature can be done in the context of the study of history, so that the characters and events are interpreted using an appropriate frame of reference. The banning of books often reflects the application of certain contemporary standards to literature, standards of which an author from the past never could have been aware. We will discuss this in more detail further on.

Fourth, through study abroad and exchange programs, we can promote the learning of foreign languages through interactions with native speakers in their cultural contexts. We suggest that many students have so much difficulty learning foreign languages not because they lack the ability but because they lack the motivation. They do not see the need to learn another language. People might be better off, we suggest, if they made more of an attempt wisely to understand other cultures rather than just to expect people from other cultures to understand them. And learning the language of a culture is a key to understanding. People might be less quick to impose their cultural values on others if they understood the others' cultures values. It is also interesting to speculate on why Esperanto, a language that was to provide a common medium of communication across cultures, has been a notable failure. We suggest it is because Esperanto is embedded in no culture at all. It is the language of no one.

Culture cannot be taught, in the context of foreign-language learning, in the way it now often is—as an aside divorced from the actual learning of the language. It should be taught as an integral part of the language—as a primary context in which the language is embedded. The vituperative fights we see about bilingual education and about use of Spanish in the US or French in Canada are not just or even primarily fights about language. They are fights about culture, and they are fights in need of wise resolutions.

Finally, as implied throughout these examples, the curriculum needs to be far more integrated. Literature needs to be integrated with history, science with history and social policy studies, foreign language with culture. Even within disciplines, far more integration is needed.

Teaching wisdom programmatically

School *can* help enhance wise thinking skills in students, and next we describe a curriculum program that we have developed to help teachers teach for wisdom.

The program reviewed here, Teaching for Wisdom, was designed to facilitate the development of wise and critical thinking skills in middle school children through the infusion of these skills into a history curriculum (Reznitskaya & Sternberg, 2004). The aim was to enhance students' wise and critical thinking skills, as well as their knowledge of American history, although the history of any other country might have been used instead. First, we examine how a theoretical model can be transcribed into guidelines for developing a classroom curriculum. We then show examples of the implementation of the curriculum in a number of public middle schools.

Teaching for Wisdom is based on Sternberg's (1998, 2001) balance theory of wisdom, reviewed above, which posits in essence that wise thinking involves the ability to use one's intelligence in the service of a common good by balancing one's own interests with those of other people and of a broader community over both the short- and long-terms. Although it is a complex model accounting for real behaviors in real contexts, it is possible to apply the theory in a concrete, real-world setting, as we have done in this program. How was it done?

We believe that the goal of teaching for wisdom can be achieved by providing students with educational contexts where students can formulate their own understanding of what constitutes wise thinking. In other words, teaching for wisdom is not accomplished through a didactic method of 'imparting' information *about wisdom* and subsequently assessing students with multiple-choice questions. Instead, students need to actively experience various cognitive and affective processes that underlie wise decision-making. In other words, teachers can provide scaffolding for the development of wisdom, but they cannot teach particular courses of actions, or give students a list of do's and don'ts, regardless of circumstances.

What then are the processes underlying wise thinking that students have to acquire, and how can they be introduced into the classroom? Sternberg (2001) outlines pedagogical principles and procedures derived from the theory of wisdom. The fundamental idea behind all these educational guidelines is that the instructor teaches children not *what* to think, but, rather, *how* to think.

Let us review here six procedures for teaching for wisdom. Many of these procedures are already in use by classroom teachers, and what we strive for in our curriculum is not so much to revolutionize teaching and make instructors rotate their educational practices 180 degrees, but rather, to help teachers systematically and frequently implement sound teaching procedures that foster wise thinking.

Procedure 1. Encourage students to read classic works of literature and philosophy (whether western or otherwise) to learn and reflect on the wisdom of the sages

The rush to dump classic works in favor of modern works makes sense only if the wisdom these modern works had to impart equaled or exceeded that of the classic works. When discussing the readings, encourage students to engage in *reflective thinking,* to reflect on their own functioning to increase their metacognition (Flavell, 1987), that is, their awareness of their cognitions, emotions and beliefs. The process of making a wise decision requires an ongoing monitoring of selected strategies, as well as an ability to modify less successful strategies to better fit the situational demands. Teachers can help students develop wise thinking by designing instructional activities that allow students to explore and shape their own values. Also, students can be explicitly instructed in useful metacognitive strategies such as self-questioning or the use of self-monitoring checklists. For example, in our history curriculum, students study the ideas of the intellectual movement of the Enlightenment and the character of Benjamin Franklin. In one activity, students first read Franklin's maxims published in *Poor Richard's almanac,* such as 'Whatever is begun in anger ends in shame', 'Be slow in choosing a friend, slower in changing', 'Well done is better than well said', etc (Franklin, 1983). Next, students work in pairs to describe to their partners their own past experiences where one of the Franklin's maxims could apply. Students are then invited to think of a maxim they have learned from their own past and to continue writing their maxims in a notebook or a journal throughout the school year. From this activity, students learn about the benefits of reflecting on one's life experiences and thinking about a general rule or maxim they can apply to new situations. Wisdom involves an ability to learn from the past, whether your own or that of other people. Reflective thinking about one's life experiences is an important skill that students get to practice in this activity. Also, having students generate their own maxims throughout the year helps to make reflection on various life experiences a habit of mind.

Procedure 2. Engage students in class discussions, projects, and essays that encourage them to discuss the lessons they have learned from the literary and philosophical works they've read, and how these lessons can be applied to their own lives and the lives of others

In our history curriculum, for example, we make salient the relationships between history and personally relevant everyday experiences. When studying the character of Benjamin Franklin, students examine his accomplishments at improving his own community, such as the establishment of a post office and a library. Students then consider the needs of their own school and classroom communities and devise a plan to address these needs. The goal of such activities is to allow students to see the relevance of historical figures and events to their own lives in order to develop their ability to benefit from past experience and to become active contributors to contemporary history.

Engagement in open discussions and school projects like the one just described should help students develop dialogical and dialectical thinking, in addition to the reflective thinking described earlier. What is dialogical thinking? When one is faced with a complex problem involving several points of view, it is often necessary to take into account different frames of reference and various perspectives to find the best possible solution. What may at first appear as the right answer may turn out to be the wrong choice when the long-term is considered, or when the interests of the community as a whole are taken into account. In dialogical thinking, one uses multiple frames of reference to generate and deliberate about various perspectives on the issue at hand. Optimal solutions come from careful weighing of alternatives, rather than from following one single prescribed course of action. In the classroom, teachers can nourish students' ability to think dialogically by proposing activities in which multiple points of view are presented and discussed. Some empirical studies that have investigated the effectiveness of student discussions for the development of dialogical thinking show improvements in students' ability to resolve ill-structured problems following their participation in the discussions (Kuhn *et al.*, 1997; Reznitskaya *et al.*, 2001). In our history curriculum, one example of an activity that fosters the development of dialogical thinking comes from the historical topic of British colonial polices in the late eighteenth century. In this activity, students read multiple accounts (primary historical sources) of events during the Boston Massacre. The reports include an excerpt from a colonial newspaper, an account by a British captain, and an interview with a Boston shoemaker. Students discuss the origins of the differences among the accounts and evaluate the relative credibility of the sources. They are also invited to write their own account of the Boston Massacre events and to consider how their own frames of reference affect their descriptions. From this activity, students learn to appreciate the importance of multiple standpoints, the constructed nature of knowledge, and the powerful influences of one's perspective on one's view of the world.

Whereas dialogical thinking involves the consideration and weighing of multiple points of view, *dialectical thinking* emphasizes the consideration and *integration* of two opposing perspectives. The first perspective considered is the *thesis*. For example, one can be a radical pacifist and opposed to any military presence or intervention, whatever the circumstances. A second perspective, an *antithesis* (a negation of the original statement) is then considered. For example, one can argue that people can only live freely and in peace if their borders are protected by armed forces. Finally, a *synthesis* or reconciliation of the two seemingly opposing statements is developed. For example, one might decide that borders under dispute should be protected by a third party, such as an international army, rather than having the opposing countries measure their military strength against each other. The process does not stop when the two opposing views are reconciled; on the contrary, each synthesis becomes a new thesis, which can then be integrated in a new round of dialectical thinking. In the classroom, dialectical thinking can be encouraged through opportunities to study different sources, enabling students to build their own knowledge, or through writing assignments that explicitly call for a thesis, antithesis, and synthesis. Empirical studies have investigated the impact of developing such a fluid and dynamic concept of knowledge, where the source of knowledge is not the 'authority' (the teacher or the book), but rather, the student. Such conceptions of knowledge have been shown to relate to active engagement in learning (see McDevitt, 1990), persistence in performing a task (see Dweck & Leggett, 1988), and deeper comprehension and integration of the material taught (see Songer & Linn, 1991; Qian & Alvermann, 2000).

An example of an activity where students get to practise their dialectical thinking in our curriculum comes from the same unit on the colonial independence movement. In this activity, students first study the writings of Thomas Paine and Charles Inglis, who express two opposing views on the question of whether America should break away from England. Next, students consider a compromise solution proposed by Joseph Galloway, who attempts to reconcile the two conflicting positions. Students then discuss the notion of compromise and propose their own resolutions to the British–American conflict. Through this activity, students practise synthesizing and reconciling opposing perspectives. They also learn to recognize that the same questions can be answered differently at different points in time.

Procedure 3. Encourage students to study not only 'truth' but values, as developed during their reflective thinking

In our curriculum, students were presented with Benjamin Franklin's maxims and encouraged to engage in reflective thinking. In the homework related to that classroom activity, students are asked to study an excerpt from Franklin's autobiography, where Franklin describes his plan to achieve moral perfection. Having read Franklin's plan, students choose three values that they consider important, and develop their own plan to improve their characters. Students then monitor their behavior for a period of one week and record in a journal their successes and failures at practising the chosen values. This activity allows students to explore, form and apply their own values. Also, students are given an opportunity to monitor events in their daily lives and to recognize the connections between values and actions.

Procedure 4. Place an increased emphasis on critical, creative, and practical thinking in the service of good ends that benefit the common good

In the typical classroom, teachers encourage critical thinking skills in their students. Some teachers also aim to develop creative and practical thinking skills (Sternberg & Grigorenko, 2000) by engaging students in activities that lead them to go beyond the content they have studied (creative thinking) in order to apply this knowledge to their environment (practical thinking). To enhance wise thinking, however, students can also be encouraged to consider the outcome of their thinking, and to keep in mind that the best solution is not the one that benefits only the individual doing the thinking, but rather the one that helps others as well. The common good should be the guiding principle in choosing between different possible solutions. For example, in another unit of our history curriculum, students study the topic of slavery in America. In one of the activities, students are encouraged to consider the various reasons underlying the choice of importing slaves to work on the sugar cane plantations. Through readings and classroom discussions, students learn about the analytical, practical, and creative reasons behind the Europeans' choice to import free labor from Africa (need for cheap labor, possibility to import free laborers from Africa who were more resistant to European diseases than Native Americans and well adapted to a tropical climate, etc). Students are led to consider and debate the analytical reasons for this choice, and shown the limitations of choices made purely on the basis of self-interest: importing free labour may have furthered the goal of increased power and financial wealth for the European settlers, but was it the best solution to the need for more plantation workers?

Procedure 5. Encourage students to think about how almost any topic they study might be used for better or worse ends, and about how important that final end is

As described under Procedure 4, students can be encouraged to seek different solutions and to choose the one that benefits the common good rather than the individual. They should also be brought to realize that, just as there are different solutions benefiting different people, a given concept or point of knowledge can be used to a good or poor end.

The end to which one chooses to apply one's knowledge matters greatly. For example, in the unit on American slavery, we ask students to consider the consequences that technological inventions, such as cotton gin, had on slaves and slave owners. Through reading and classroom discussions, students learn that while the cotton gin increased the prosperity of the plantation owners, it also led to the intensification of slavery and increased human suffering. In the related activity, students discuss the values that underlie past and present choices of technology. For example, students realize that when choosing fast food or microwaves, we value time and cost over food quality and health, or when driving cars we implicitly value convenience and time over safety and environment. Thus, students become aware of the multiple consequences of given decisions, and learn to analyze their own choices in relation to a variety of interests and goals.

Procedure 6. Remember that a teacher is a role model

To role model wisdom, the teacher adopts a Socratic approach to teaching, and invites students to play a more active role in constructing learning—from their own point of view and from that of others. Wise thinking is not a set of rules or decisions that the teacher can outline for students to copy down; it is a type of thinking that the students themselves need to adopt and master. The most effective way to encourage wise thinking skills is not through memory drills but through student participation and teacher modeling. For example, a teacher can capitalize on a negative event, such as two students getting into a fight, as a way to demonstrate how one can approach a similar situation in a more constructive way. The teacher can model wise thinking by saying:

> When I get into the situations like this, I try to see the dispute from the perspective of the other person and think about whether my own behavior contributed to the situation. Was there anything I could have done differently to prevent this confrontation? Is there a solution to our disagreement that is acceptable to both of us?

Also, teachers may wish not to miss the opportunity to recognize and praise good judgments made by students, such as when they show consideration for others and their ideas, or when they offer a solution that benefits the class as a whole rather than themselves as individuals. The most effective teacher is likely to be one who can create a classroom community in which wisdom is practised, rather than preached. Wisdom can be attained in real life and not just on paper, and it can lead to a more harmonious existence.

The examples we have cited to show how the principles of the balance theory of wisdom can be applied to instruction and infused into a curriculum are all excerpts from two units we developed for use in middle school US history classrooms.[1] While we chose to integrate the teaching for wisdom into a subject matter of history, we do not believe that wisdom is limited to history—wise thinking skills can be infused in most subject areas and at most grade levels. While researchers are still trying to determine at which age children are able to engage in higher-order thinking (see Stein & Miller, 1993), we observed that most of the procedures described here can be adapted from at least the end of elementary school. Let us briefly review how the procedures and principles for wise thinking can be used in other subject areas, as discussed earlier in this text.

In science teaching, dialectical thinking can be applied to illustrate to students the notion that scientific facts are not eternal or immutable, but rather the state of affairs as we perceive them at this very specific point in time. How many scientists in his time considered as scientific evidence the data presented by Galileo Galilei to demonstrate that the Earth revolved around the Sun, and not vice versa? Students also need to understand that scientific method is susceptible to being subverted by ideology or considerations of political expediency, as in case of the Soviet biologist Trofim Lysenko. Ostensibly following strict scientific procedures Lysenko, in fact, manufactured results to align them with the ideological postulates and expectations of the Communist Party leadership.

Wise thinking skills can also be applied in the literature classroom. Literature is often taught in terms of the standards and context of the contemporary American scene. Characters often are judged in terms of our contemporary standards rather than in terms of the standards of the time and place in which the events took place. One example is the opposition by a parent from an Arizona school district to the study of Mark Twain's *Huckleberry Finn* in her daughter's high school English class because the book contains the word 'nigger'. The parent felt that this would exacerbate already existing racial tensions in the school. In the words of Circuit Judge Reinhard, who ruled on the case:

> The setting is a freshman English class in Tempe, Arizona, and the competing interests are the First Amendment rights of high school students to receive information or ideas—even when contained in literary works that may in today's world appear to have racist overtones—and the rights of those same students to receive a public education that neither fosters nor acquiesces in a racially hostile environment. (Monteiro *vs.* Tempe Union High School District, 97-15511, U.S. 9th Circuit Court of Appeals, October 19, 1998)

The Appeals Court eventually ruled against the banning of books.

The foreign language classroom is another terrain for enhancing students' wise thinking skills. Foreign languages should be taught in the cultural context in which they are embedded, requiring students to engage in reflective and dialogical thinking to grasp the foreign culture and to position themselves and their experiences in relation to this culture. It tends to be more common in Europe to speak one or several languages beyond one's mother tongue. Perhaps American students have so much more difficulty learning foreign languages than do children in much of Europe not because they lack the ability, but because they lack the motivation and the exposure. An American student would probably much more readily see the need to learn a foreign language if each of the 50 states spoke a different language, much like the member states of the European Union do. We would also do our students a service by teaching them to understand other cultures rather than just to expect people from other cultures to understand them. Learning the language of a culture is a key to understanding it, and the two cannot be taught separately or by viewing culture as an appendix to language rather than the context in which it is deeply rooted. Wise people understand not only their own culture, but other cultures, and learning languages helps us achieve such understanding.

Conclusion

The road to this new approach to education, via the balance theory of wisdom, is bound to be a rocky one. First, entrenched structures, whatever they may be, are difficult to change, and wisdom is neither taught in schools nor, in general, is it even discussed. Second, many people will not see the value of teaching something that shows no promise of raising conventional test scores. These scores, which formerly were predictors of more interesting criteria, have now become criteria, or ends, in themselves. Society has lost track of why they ever mattered in the first place and they have engendered the same kind of mindless competition we see in people who relentlessly compare their economic achievements with those of others. Third, wisdom is much more difficult to develop than is the kind of achievement that can be developed and then readily tested via multiple-choice tests. Finally, people who have gained influence and power in a society via one means are unlikely to want either to give up that power or to see a new criterion be established on which they do not rank as favorably.

There is no easy road to wisdom. There never was, and probably never will be. As an educational system, we have turned on the easy road, but the wrong road. It is not too late to turn back. By ratcheting up our emphasis on a narrow conception of what it means to be a 'good student', we are ignoring the broader conception that will make a difference to individuals and society. It is not merely what we know, but how we use it, that will determine the fate of our society and of others.

Acknowledgements

Preparation of this article was supported by a grant from the W. T. Grant Foundation. Grantees undertaking such projects are encouraged to express freely their professional judgment. This article, therefore, does not necessarily represent the positions or the policies of the W. T. Grant Foundation.

Notes

1. Additional information on these units can be obtained by visiting the PACE web site at http://pace.tufts.edu/, or by sending an inquiry to robert.sternberg@tufts.edu.

Notes on contributors

Robert J. Sternberg is Dean of the School of Arts and Sciences at Tufts University.
Linda Jarvin is Adjunct Associate Professor and Deputy Director of the Center for the Psychology of Abilities, Competencies, and Expertise at Tufts University.
Alina Reznitskaya is Assistant Professor of Psychology at Montclair State University.

References

Baltes, P. B. & Smith, J. (in press) *Wisdom: the orchestration of mind and virtue* (Boston, Blackwell).
Dweck, C. S. & Leggett, E. L. (1988) A social–cognitive approach to motivation and personality, *Psychological Review*, 95, 256–273.
Flavell, J. H. (1987) Speculations about the nature and development of metacognition, in: F. E. Wienert & R. H. Kluwe (Eds) *Metacognition, motivation, and understanding* (Hillsdale, NJ, Erlbaum), 21–29.
Flynn, J. R. (1998) IQ gains over time: toward finding the causes, in: U. Neisser (Ed.) *The rising curve: long-term gains in IQ and related measures* (Washington, DC, American Psychological Association), 25–66.
Franklin, B. (1983) *Poor Richard's almanac* (White Plains, NY, Peter Pauper Press). (Original work published 1733, 1749, 1756, 1757, 1758.)
Gardner, H. (1983) *Frames of mind: the theory of multiple intelligences* (New York, Basic Books).
Hegel, G. W. F. (1931) *The phenomenology of the mind* (London, Allen & Unwin). (Original work published 1807.)
Herrnstein, R. J. & Murray, C. (1994) *The bell curve* (New York, Free Press).
Kuhn, D., Shaw, V. & Felton, M. (1997) Effects of dyadic interaction on argumentative reasoning, *Cognition and Instruction*, 15, 287–315.

McDevitt, T. M. (1990) Mothers' and children's beliefs about listening, *Child Study Journal*, 20, 105–128.

Neisser, U. (Ed.) (1998) *The rising curve* (Washington, DC, American Psychological Association).

Qian, G. & Alvermann, D. E. (2000) Relationship between epistemological beliefs and conceptual change learning, *Reading and Writing Quarterly*, 16, 59–74.

Reznitskaya, A., Anderson, R. C., McNurlen, B., Nguyen-Jahiel, K., Archodidou, A. & Kim, S. (2001) Influence of oral discussion on written argument, *Discourse Processes*, 32, 155–175.

Reznitskaya, A. & Sternberg, R. J. (2004) Teaching students to make wise judgments: the 'teaching for wisdom' program, in: P. A. Linley & S. Joseph (Eds) *Positive psychology in practice* (New York, Wiley), 181–196.

Songer, N. B. & Linn, M. C. (1991) How do views of science influence knowledge integration, *Journal of Research in Science Teaching*, 28, 761–784.

Stein, N. L. & Miller, C. A. (1993) A theory of argumentative understanding: relationships among position preference, judgments of goodness, memory, and reasoning, *Argumentation*, 7, 183–204.

Sternberg, R. J. (1985) *Beyond IQ: a triarchic theory of human intelligence* (New York, Cambridge University Press).

Sternberg, R. J. (Ed.) (1990) *Wisdom: its nature, origins, and development* (New York, Cambridge University Press).

Sternberg, R. J. (1997) *Successful intelligence* (New York, Plume).

Sternberg, R. J. (1998a) A balance theory of wisdom, *Review of General Psychology*, 2, 347–365.

Sternberg, R. J. (1998b) The dialectic as a tool for teaching psychology, *Teaching of Psychology*, 25, 177–180.

Sternberg, R. J. (2001) Why schools should teach for wisdom: the balance theory of wisdom in educational settings, *Educational Psychologist*, 36(4), 227–245.

Sternberg, R. J. (Ed.) (2002) *Why smart people can be so stupid* (New Haven, CT, Yale University Press).

Sternberg, R. J. (2003) A duplex theory of hate: development and application to terrorism, massacres, and genocide, *Review of General Psychology*, 7(3), 299–328.

Sternberg, R. J. & Grigorenko, E. L. (2002) *Teaching for successful intelligence* (Arlington Heights, IL, Skylight).

Sternberg, R. J. & Jordan, J. (Eds.) (2005) *Handbook of wisdom: psychological perspectives* (New York, Cambridge University Press).

Webster's new world dictionary (1997) *Webster's new world dictionary* (New York, Simon & Schuster).

Wisdom and lifelong learning in the twenty-first century

Richard Hawley Trowbridge

Introduction

It may be that today we are in the same relation to wisdom as *Homo erectus* was to language: we have barely started down the path. Much of our knowledge about Earth, the universe, life and human development is very new. In a universe where time is measured in intervals of a million years, it might be wise to consider that the great teachers throughout history did not provide final truths, but way stations at the beginning of a long journey. The level of human wisdom is indicated by the wars *Homo sapiens* is presently undertaking, and the money being spent on weapons compared with that spent on cultivating mental and physical wellness. A further gauge is the extent to which the average human attains full cognitive, emotional, social, and spiritual potential. We seem closer to a barbarian than to a sage society.

As a value or as a topic of academic interest, wisdom had been all but forgotten in the West until around the time of Gabriel Marcel's *The decline of wisdom* (1955). New perspectives on wisdom from philosophy (e.g., virtue ethics) then began to come forth; and new perspectives from theology, with rediscovered interest in the sapiential tradition. In psychology, the empirical study of wisdom began in the 1970s. On wisdom's return, we discern in it features that don't seem to have been present in earlier eras.

Although it has been hardly heard from for over 200 years, it is clear that wisdom has not become a period-piece but has kept pace with the advance of scientific knowledge. Wisdom is discussed in terms of such up-to-the-minute concepts as postformal thought, metacognition, and emotional and social intelligence. Wisdom assumed without delay its place as the integrating and all-encompassing concept for higher order mental, social and spiritual virtues (Baltes & Staudinger, 2000; Baltes, 2004)—an updated statement of the ancient formula, *sapientiae est ordinare*. Certainly an attractive topic given the global problematique.

Much of the recent academic discussion of wisdom concerns its nature and definition. (In a later section of this article—'Wisdom and Skill'—a definition is provided.) This is a necessary and instructive exercise, but whatever 'wisdom' means, and conceding that we will never be wise, there is evidence that many individuals, and humanity in general, can make transformational progress in becoming wiser, in a short time. If this is to occur, one key may be to bring quality programs for developing wisdom to lifelong learning centers for older adults. This article presents: (1) an overview of demographics of the ageing population; (2) developmental possibilities for matured people, and their relation to wisdom; (3) a survey of courses related to wisdom in lifelong learning programs for older people; (4) a description of the Wisdom as Skill program; (5) concluding thoughts.

Demographics of an ageing population

For most of the twentieth century, there was little interest in older people by psychologists, and less recognition that ageing provides possibilities beyond decline. James E. Birren, one of the first to take a more positive approach, points out (1999, p. 460) that scientific study of ageing began in the late twentieth century. Due in large part to demographics and finances, this period of neglect is rapidly ending. There are 76 million residents of the US who are 'baby-boomers', born between 1946–1964, slightly over 25% of the US population. The generation senior to them consists of 59 million living people in the US; together these generations are changing the center of demographic gravity in this country. In the UK (England and Wales), almost 40% of the population was 45-years-old or older in 2001 (Office of National Statistics, 2001, Table KS02). 'As we begin the twenty-first century', Kinsella and Velcoff (2001, pp. 1, 3) point out, 'population aging is poised to emerge as a preeminent worldwide phenomenon. … The coming growth, especially of the oldest old [i.e., over 80-years-old], will be stunning'.

Until living memory, the average length of life did not extend far beyond childbearing and -raising years. In the UK and in the US, average expected lifespan at birth has risen 30 years since 1900. In a recent *New York Times* article describing the dramatic improvements in health among older people (Kolata, 2006), the University of Chicago's Robert W. Fogel is quoted as observing that advances in longevity and health in the past hundred years are 'unique among the 7000 or so generations of humans who have ever inhabited the earth'. While this cohort is larger in the US than elsewhere, the number of old people alive today worldwide is greater than ever, and they are better educated, healthier, more active, and better-off financially than the old have ever been (David, 2001, p. 130). Characteristics of this unique cohort seem to provide an opportunity for creating a wiser global community, and for working out effective methods for facilitating attainment of optimal human development.

The material abundance lavished upon a large number of people in the second half of the twentieth century allowed a more expansive view of human nature and human potentials to come forth. Regarding physical and mental health, after the Second World War attention has focused increasingly on prevention relative to cure, and in healthy development relative to pathology (World Health Organization, 1948). True, Ryff and Singer could observe in 1998 (p. 1) that 'there has been no discernible progress in carrying these views to the scientific or practice realms'. But by now it has become possible to describe what amounts to a new dimension of human development, a new awareness utilizing many higher-order mental activities: metacognition, emotional and social intelligence, self-knowledge in depth, autonomy and interrelatedness, critical thinking. All these higher-order skills are integrated in wisdom. The psychological research of the past 30 years has permitted a science-based description of wisdom to be articulated, and steps to learning it have been hewn out. Great numbers of people in the 'developed' world are entering old age still healthy, technologically savvy and educated. They face the challenge of major life changes, as their children leave home and they leave their jobs. These challenges call for wisdom, a quality long associated with people who have lived long and seen much. Only recently have psychologists begun to recognize positive developmental possibilities for older people, often using the term wisdom to denote fulfillment of these potentials.

Developmental tasks and possibilities for older people

In 1991, Baltes *et al.* (pp. 127–128) wrote 'It is possible … that the present-day cultural construction of human aging is akin to that of an underdeveloped, relatively 'illiterate' society' and that contemporary developmental scientists may have only a slight idea of what the possibilities for development in old age might be. This suggestion was echoed by feminist author Betty Friedan (1993, p. 87):

> We have barely even considered the possibilities in age for new kinds of loving intimacy, purposeful work and activity, learning and knowing, community and care. … For to see age as continued human development involves a revolutionary paradigm shift.

The years since these evaluations were made have been a time of extraordinary advances. Understanding of the ageing mind-brain has been revolutionized during and after the Decade of the Brain, an initiative of the US Library of Congress and the National Institute of Mental Health, which lasted throughout the 1990s. Much research on continuing development throughout the lifespan has been conducted, and many approaches tried.

Possibly the most influential model of human development in the twentieth century was Jean Piaget's (1932, 1966), which is restricted to intellectual and moral development and stops with the development of ability to carry out 'formal operations' in adolescence. Sigmund Freud's (1935) model of psychosexual development likewise ends in adolescence with the 'genital stage' of maturing sexual interest.

Erik Erikson (1950), whose work was based on the psychoanalytic theory of Freud, provided the first (and still dominant) model of psychosocial development to extend throughout the lifespan. The last two of his eight stages ('tasks' has been suggested as a preferable term) involve the development of care—'a widening commitment to *take care of* the persons, the products, and the ideas one has learned *to care for*' (1997, p. 67)—and wisdom through successfully resolving the choices of generativity versus stagnation, and integrity versus despair. In fact, empirical study of wisdom began with the questioning of this model (Clayton, 1975, 1976. Erikson did not mention wisdom until the second edition, 1963).

In his presentation of the results of the lengthiest observations of lifelong development, the Study of Adult Development at Harvard University, George Vaillant (2002, p. 40) follows a revised Eriksonian model for *Aging well* (the title of the book), adding a Freudian element of mature defense mechanisms. His research led him to concur with Erikson's identification of a widening circle of concern with increasing age (p. 44). This is observed particularly in the achievement of generativity: caring for the future of the larger community as well as passing along individually acquired learning. Vaillant describes the four 'critical components' of the latter years of life as maintaining a sense of well-being despite illness; creativity and playfulness; acquiring wisdom; and cultivating spirituality (p. 37).

Since the 1970s, Piaget's model has been augmented by psychologists who consider additional life domains than he did, and recognize the occurrence of mental development beyond the mastery of formal operations. Later development has the goal of meshing the individual with his or her larger context, and achieving a sense of meaning, according to Jan Sinnott. Mastering postformal operations allows 'for conscious orchestration of emotional and cognitive life, leading to emotional self-regulation … maturity, and wisdom' (1998, p. 55). Neopiagetian Juan Pascual-Leone believes that wisdom is 'the ultimate possible achievement of a normal person's growth'. It is the integration of the totality of a person's being, when it 'reaches sufficient breadth and cohesiveness', that allows wisdom to appear (1990, p. 245).

Two earlier psychological models of late life development can be mentioned. Carl Jung distinguished two stages in the lifecourse: during the first half, the individual's task is to establish him- or herself in the outer world, attaining a developed ego. In the second half of life, one goes within, seeking integration and harmony, ideally 'building up a state of wider and higher consciousness' (Jung, 1969, p. 393) beyond the perspective of the individual organism. More recently, Jung's observation that with ageing there is a shift from extraversion to introversion has been confirmed by Chris Beckett (2002, p. 200). Beckett observes that this growing inwardness corresponds to Erikson's view of the tasks of later life. Much in agreement with Jung's position, Harry R. Moody claims that 'In psychodynamic terms, the process of life review constitutes the major developmental task of old age, and it is the fundamental question for any philosophy of aging' (1978, p. 34). In his experience, Moody, whose career has been spent in studying the psychology of old people, has 'always found' a desire of old people to tell their story, to make sense of their experience.

Abraham Maslow's concept of self-actualization, while considered to be a lifelong process, was reserved for older people. 'In our culture at least, youngsters have not yet achieved identity, or autonomy … nor have they generally become knowledgeable and educated enough to open the possibility of becoming wise' (1970, p. xx). Maslow believed that only 1% of the population was self-actualizing (1968, p. 204). Many are unable to self-actualize due to economic and social barriers raised against people of their gender, religion and race. It should be clear that in contemporary society few will achieve the development of wisdom. It is worth entertaining Maslow's estimate that, as Ruth Cox mentions in her 'Afterword' to the third edition of *Motivation and personality* (1987, p. 263) 'a society with 8 percent self-actualizing people would soon be a self-actualizing society'.

Current models of healthy ageing present two distinct views on optimal development in the latter years of the lifespan, which can be designated as successful ageing and conscious ageing. Both contribute to optimal ageing: the former to optimization of one's physical and mental abilities in the face of age-related decline, and the latter to finding meaning in one's life and place in the universe, and accepting decline and mortality. Successful ageing, as described by Rowe and Kahn (1998) in presenting the results of the MacArthur Founda-tion Study of Aging in America, is characterized by low risk of disease, high mental and physical functioning, and active engagement with life. Success means continuing to function at optimal physical and mental level; wisdom is not necessarily involved. Conscious ageing, on the other hand, requires a long, arduous effort to go beyond the ego structures one has built throughout a lifetime to find a home for one's identity in a larger, transpersonal entity. H. R. Moody (2003, p. 143) states that 'World wisdom traditions regard this course of transcendence as a human being's struggle to overcome the self'. While conscious ageing includes the Eriksonian challenge of achieving integrity versus declining into despair, its ego transcendence aspect is not part of Erikson's model. Moody predicts that success-ful ageing will appeal to more people, as it aligns well with cultural values of success, productivity and youth. It does not require a reevaluation of one's identity or values.

The accuracy of Moody's view appears from an analysis of major policy reports in the UK on lifelong education, which 'reveals a strong priority accorded to vocational educa-tion and training in spite of some general rhetoric about the non-economic, personal and social benefits of lifelong learning' (Withnall, 2000). Richard Taylor (2005, p. 104) concludes that 'the whole thrust of the Labour Government's policy [regarding lifelong learning] has been market oriented'. In the US, a recent report in the *New York Times* (Olson, 2006) discusses the role of community colleges in providing ongoing education for baby boomers in their retirement. The colleges appear entirely focused on helping provide 'the credentials and training they will need to reposition themselves for second careers'. This is prototypical successful ageing. An elegant heuristic for successful ageing that applies to at least some aspects of wisdom is provided by leading geropsychologist Paul B. Baltes' model of 'selection, optimization, and compensation' (Baltes & Freund, 2003; Baltes *et al.*, 2005).

A model of conscious ageing is Lars Tornstam's (1997) gerotranscendence, which he regards as 'the final stage in a natural progression towards maturation and wisdom'. Tornstam describes gerotranscendence as a shift to a transpersonal perspective, with intrapersonal, interpersonal, and cosmic aspects.

The distinction made between instrumental and expressive activities (Havighurst, 1976; Londoner, 1978), often used for describing the motivations of older learners, is similar to that between successful and conscious ageing. Instrumental activities are those engaged in for the sake of achieving an external goal, usually in the future. Expressive activities are pursued for their intrinsic satisfaction. Manheimer's distinction between adaptational and transformational theories of development (Manheimer et al., 1995) is also comparable to the successful–conscious division.

The possibilities for continuing mental development in later years rest on a distinction between fluid and crystallized intelligence. The former refers to the speed and accuracy of mental processes, the latter to acquired knowledge and its successful application. While in activities depending on fluid intelligence performance has been found to decline with age, in those utilizing crystallized intelligence, ageing can correlate with improved performance. Although in their research Paul B. Baltes and his colleagues have found that increasing age generally does not correlate with increasing wisdom-related performance, or WRP (Staudinger, 1999, p. 660), older people are disproportionately represented among the highest scorers on their tests for measuring WRP. A useful finding of their research is that increasing age has both wisdom-increasing and wisdom-diminishing potentials. Greater experience and personal growth facilitate increases in wisdom, while declines in cognitive abilities, decrease in openness to new experience, and greater mental rigidity act against the increase of wisdom (Staudinger, 1999). It is research into crystallized intelligence, or 'cognitive pragmatics', that led to the pioneering empirical study of wisdom by Baltes and his colleagues at the Max Planck Institute for Human Development and Education (Baltes, 1993, p. 585).

The possibilities for psychosocial development in old age according to these sources can be summarized as:

- Enduring illness and loss without undue diminishment of activity and good spirits;
- A widening circle of caring for and taking care of.
- Post-formal thought—recognition of the validity of differing reality systems, and monitoring and regulating thoughts and emotions.
- Self-actualization (including creativity, a sense of play, learning how to live well).
- Deepening self-knowledge, integrating all aspects of one's person, setting the personal self in a larger context and identifying with that context.
- Gaining of wisdom, the culmination of human development.

To what extent does this occur? Particularly the last three achievements, which require a good deal of introspection and reflection? It is a worthwhile question to ask, as the advent of great numbers of older people, for the first time in history, offers the opportunity to discover and encourage their full psychosocial maturation. Such development will in turn promote more sustainable economic practices, and long-term and holistic perspectives, benefiting the entire human community. Post-baby boom generations may have to cope with a lowered standard of living, environmental crises and violent global conflicts. Marcel (1955), noting the neglect of wisdom in the modern world, suggested that the concurrent devaluing of older people 'is undoubtedly connected with the devaluation suffered by wisdom itself' (p. 40). This might be the opportune moment to change the low regard in which elders have been held in industrial societies, and assist people in older years find a role as stewards and transmitters of more thoughtful and encompassing cultural values. There is ample reason to link wisdom promotion with ongoing psychosocial development of older people.

Lifelong learning for the elderly

Jung, Erikson and Tornstam may be correct in maintaining that there is a natural tendency to turn inward and grow wiser as one approaches death; but it is not likely that this can be accomplished optimally without guidance. There is little social support for accomplishing tasks such as deepening self-knowledge, achieving ego-integration and -transcendence, and gaining wisdom; and expecting older people to do so on their own is unrealistic. One venue for instruction in the requisite skills is learning in retirement centers. These are a relatively recent phenomenon, whose history beyond the forerunner stage dates to the 1970s. In this section I examine the existence of wisdom-oriented groups in two such institutions: the University of the Third Age (U3A) in the UK, and in Institutes for Lifelong Learning (ILLs) in the US.

The University of the Third Age began in France in the early 1970s, utilizing university sites and resources to offer summer courses for retired people. This proved popular, and in 1981 the first U3A in Britain was established at Cambridge. It was decided that restriction to university sites was too limiting, and subsequently U3As were set up wherever enough people were interested. Today there are 614 U3As in the UK, and over 167,000 members (U3A & Third Age Trust, 2007). They offer ongoing groups, as well as one-time events, in which volunteer members share their knowledge and experience. All people of appropriate age are welcome to participate, and often the quality of the groups is high— for example, organized by people who were professionally involved in the areas covered. For this study I searched the web pages of 145 such U3As, to identify all the ongoing groups (about 4300) and those focused on wisdom, and more broadly, on areas of self-development such as psychology and philosophy.

Institutes for Lifelong Learning began in 1962 with the Institute for Retired Professionals at Manhattan's New School for Social Research. By the late 1970s there were half a dozen such organizations. In the late 1980s, Elderhostel (which itself began in 1975) formed a network for such organizations, almost all of which are sponsored by universities and colleges, and usually offer participants access to the school's resources. Today there are over 300 member organizations of the Elderhostel Institute Network (EIN) and an estimated 500 such ILLs throughout North America (Elderhostel, 2007). I searched the web pages of all EIN affiliated organizations with a website, identifying those courses focused on wisdom or self-development among the roughly 6000 courses at 193 such Institutes.

The review of 145 U3A centers found 54 centers with at least one group (a total of 72 groups) with either a definite or possible relation to wisdom, or personal development towards wisdom. Groups are formed according to members' interest, so the presence or absence of wisdom-oriented groups is at least an indication of what the members, who may be considered above average in their interest in learning, find important. There are 21 groups which appear to be definitely oriented toward wisdom or wisdom-related concerns; for 39 of the 72 no details are provided (including 26 philosophy groups). In identifying wisdom-oriented groups, I tried to err on the side of inclusion. Most of the 4300 groups are engaged in language study, music appreciation or performance, health concerns and physical activities, arts and crafts, and history and current events. No doubt

I have failed to include some groups that are connected with wisdom or personal development, but the conclusion is inescapable that, at least in their U3A participation, U3A members are far more interested in externally focused, objective activities than in development of abilities concerned with wisdom, self-transformation, or explicit personal development.

The same holds for ILLs in the US. Of the roughly 6000 classes or activities in 193 different ILLs, I found 181 wisdom- or personal development-related classes offered in 81 different institutions.

These findings raise a question concerning the claim that people tend to turn inward as they age. It may be naïve to expect that people in our societies, who get little experience with introspection for the first 50 years of their lives, would be able to respond adeptly to any urges in later life toward introspection, life review, or the development of wisdom. Coleman (2005, p. 304), points out that life review, requiring skilled introspection, may not be an activity most people engage in. It is certainly unrealistic to expect them to be able to do so as productively as they would if trained in reflective thinking.

If there is this small number of groups or courses for wisdom or explicit self-development in these centers, where participants set the curriculum, the conclusion has to be either that older people don't want self-development, or they don't want self-development in this context. Perhaps they are getting it indirectly through the other courses or groups—the humanities courses, discussion groups, walking groups, social activities—or in other venues. The 'self-help' section of bookstores is certainly filled with bestsellers that are wisdom-related at least in the broad sense followed in this study. In its study of the baby boomers, the American Association of Retired People (AARP, 2005) reported that less than a third of the respondents were very satisfied with their leisure activities. Leisure activities and religious or spiritual life were the areas in which improvement is most desired (pp. 43–46). This would seem to indicate potential interest in wisdom development.

Yet the older people actively pursuing lifelong learning in ILLs or the U3A do not appear very concerned with wisdom: it seems that the proportion of wisdom-oriented classes would be just as large in groups of people in their 40s, 30s, or 20s. Not what one would expect from reading Erikson or Jung.

Kim and Merriam (2004) note that there have been few studies on motives of older people for participating in learning activities. In their citations, the most recently published, before their own survey administered to 189 participants in a learning in retirement (LIR) institute, is 1993. Kim and Merriam found cognitive interest to be a significantly greater motivation than the other three factors contained in their study (social contact, family togetherness, social stimulation). In discussing the research on motivations for participation in institutes for LIR, Martin (2003, p. 3) observes that 'cognitive interests always prove to be the strongest motivator, followed by a desire for socialization'.

An examination of courses and groups in LIRs, and of studies on motivations of older people for participating in formal learning activities, do not take us very far in identifying their developmental needs. In any case, as these needs may be dimly sensed and receive little encouragement in society, the only way to identify them might be to begin with a theory and then to test it in the real world.

Alternatively, the needs can be identified by monitoring the interests actually demonstrated by older people, particularly their self-chosen informal learning, outside of enrollment in college courses or participation in LIRs. Yet this still leaves out that which people desire but are unable to articulate. In focus group interviews with 45 long-term members of an LLI, Lamb and Brady (2005) found 'opportunities for spiritual renewal' to be one of four major categories of perceived benefits—a result unanticipated by them. A straw in the wind, this finding supports the ideas of Jung and Erikson in regard to the developmental tasks of older people.

It should also be noted that most of the self-development/wisdom courses offered in ILLs are of limited duration, often no more than one to three sessions—a limitation that may account to some extent for the lack of wisdom focused courses. It's hard to go far in such a short time. (Many self-development/wisdom courses continue for eight weeks or so.) But dissatisfaction with course length would not seem to be a major factor. Language courses lasting eight weeks or less are popular; analogously, partial coverage of wisdom should be of interest—if people were interested in wisdom at all. And the U3A groups are ongoing. Perhaps the people who are working consciously toward wisdom are not those who participate in lifelong learning groups?

Or perhaps what is missing are models for a course in wisdom development. Manheimer *et al.* (1995, pp. 21–22) note the skepticism originally expressed toward offering a federally funded humanities reading and discussion group series at senior centers (as being too advanced for the population), and their subsequent widespread popularity. Wisdom may be a goal toward which older people tend; but having become rather remote from common discourse, wisdom may need an accessible program to get the ball rolling. In facilitating courses on wisdom at learning in retirement centers, I have found considerable interest in the subject, and that participants are genuinely interested in the application of wisdom in their own lives. From reviewing the literature on older people's developmental needs and their motives for participation in learning activities, it appears likely that a course on wisdom will be most successful by also responding to elders' interest in cognitive enrichment and social participation. Such a program will be helpful both in elders' search for meaning and in providing a tool for optimal resolution of problems they encounter, meeting both instrumental and expressive goals.

Wisdom really needs better marketing. It would also help to have practical programs offering direct and immediate application of wisdom behaviours and attitudes in participants' own lives. It would help if participants could gauge the success and progress of their efforts. The rest of this article is devoted to a description of the program Wisdom as Skill: Developing and Living by a Wisdom Perspective (also referred to as The Wisdom-Centered Life). Perhaps this description will inspire others to develop similar, or better, programs. Wisdom as Skill is still very much in its initial stage: in summer 2007 it will be offered for the third time.

Wisdom as Skill

Wisdom as Skill is based on the empirical studies of wisdom and its ontogenesis (Trowbridge, 2005), the philosophic tradition of cultivating wisdom (see Hadot, 2002), and models of skill development (Dreyfus & Dreyfus, 1986, 2004). The first attempt to put it into practice was made in autumn 2006 at a learning in retirement institution in western New York State.

In Wisdom as Skill, wisdom is defined as profound understanding of the basic realities of existence, living in alignment with them, and making the best possible choices conformant with this understanding. Basic realities of existence refer to, for example, suffering and death, good and evil; aesthetic appreciation of the world; the limits of human knowledge and emotional sensitivity; the natural tendency to perceive the world from a self-centered perspective; transcendence of the individual; recognition of basic equalities among all beings; possibilities of love and of awareness, happiness and misery. The definition is intended to be generic and traditional; participants are encouraged to adapt the definition, as long as it is clear what they mean by wisdom. A large collection of definitions and descriptions of wisdom that have been set forth throughout history is made available in the manual accompanying the course. About two dozen men and women participated in each of the first two courses, and there was ongoing discussion of the nature of wisdom as it appeared in participants' own lives.

The program consists of three main activities: (1) learning about wisdom; (2) developing and living by a wisdom perspective; and (3) practice with situations in the participant's own life in which she or he wants to exercise wisdom. 'Situations' is used in a broad sense, to include general reflections on one's progress toward wisdom and developing richer understanding of the meaning of existence.

Learning involves immersion in the religious, philosophical, and psychological literature on wisdom, and acquainting oneself with people or groups of people who manifest or manifested wisdom. The goal is to understand wisdom as described or exhibited by people who have dedicated much time to it. The assumption is that wisdom tends to be vaguely understood, and that a person's ability to embody and exhibit wisdom is limited by his or her clarity regarding what it is. To avoid confusion, it appears important to stress the evolving meanings of wisdom—wisdom as portrayed in the Old Testament, for example, is different from that of ancient or modern philosophers, contemporary psychologists, and even modern theologians.

Developing and living a wisdom perspective is accomplished by internalizing a number of principles, by learning and practising the character traits associated with wisdom (e.g., openness, reflectiveness, empathy, fairness and sound judgment, serenity, humor, self-knowledge, humility, a transpersonal perspective), and engaging in daily exercises. Following a hint by Hadot (2002, p. 244), a number of principles were collected; these are to be used for reflection, and to be internalized by participants.

For practising wisdom in life situations, the participant selects situations in his or her own life in which she or he would like to manifest greater wisdom. Attempts to do so are recorded in a journal, excerpts of which can be shared in small group activities (reflective case study), with a coach, or used for individual practice. As in models of expertise development, it is considered that optimal progress will be made by working on those areas that are just beyond the participant's current level of competence.

A rubric is provided by which efforts can be assessed by peers, by the individual, or by trained evaluators. Assessment is made according to six criteria (openness, centeredness and self-knowledge, reflection and holism, humility, empathy, rationality) that elaborate a single encompassing standard—the extent to which the response exemplifies and aligns with profound understanding of reality and represents the best possible choice in the situation in the light of this reality. There is a significant amount of overlap among the criteria. After assessing the belief or choice according to the criteria, its alignment with the encompassing standard is evaluated. The goal is that assessment should be as simple as possible while adequately assessing wisdom as defined.

As 'profound understanding of reality' is a matter of interpretation, and there is room for people who may be considered wise to hold quite different views regarding the nature of reality, the solution seems to lie in setting forth (1) the context of assumptions; (2) the manner in which one explores the nature of reality; and (3) the claims one makes regarding validity. Particular conclusions are subordinate—granted that it is the conclusions people have to live with.

It is likely that progress will be optimal when a person works with a partner, in a small group, or in a class conducted by a trained instructor; but working alone can be completely satisfactory.

Conclusion

For the first time in history, the balance of human interest is inclining toward the latter half of the uncurtailed lifespan. This half falls within the province of wisdom, at least potentially. Seventy-five million baby boomers in the US are entering the years during which a person naturally becomes very interested in the quality of life, in making sense of life, and in contributing positively to future generations.

Whether by chance or by necessity, it has only been in recent decades that wisdom has ceased to 'vanish almost entirely from the philosophical map' (Smith, *Routledge encyclopedia of philosophy*, 1998) and from the map of human interests altogether. Interest in wisdom on the part of the public is growing, accompanied by burgeoning interest from researchers. *Philosophers' index* lists 115 articles with wisdom as subject between 1940–1959; 220 between 1960–1979; 161 between 1980–1989; 238 between 1990–1999; 192 between 2000 and listings as of December 2006. PsychInfo finds one article with wisdom as keyword between 1940–1959; seven between 1960–1979; 13 between 1980-1989; 57 between 1990–1999; 174 from 2000 to December 2006 (searches made December, 2006).

This interest is spurred not only by a huge approaching wave of vital old people, but also by social-economic conditions that demand more complex, higher-order mental functions, such as metacognition, emotional intelligence, reflective learning, critical thinking, and postformal thought. Higher-order mental functions, too, are within the domain of wisdom, which has been conceptualized as a metaheuristic for orchestrating mind and virtue toward excellence (Baltes & Staudinger, 2000, p. 127). A wisdom perspective is the potential integrator of all input, evaluator of options, goals, and values, and planner and conductor of behaviour.

The revolutionary implications of a progression toward wisdom need to be emphasized. In the inaugural edition of the *Journal of Transpersonal Psychology*, Abraham Maslow wrote (1969, p. 6) that 'We are dealing with a new image of man'. This recalls the words of pioneer psychologist G. Stanley Hall, who, at the end of his life, expressed his conviction that 'nature is trying to bring into the world a new and higher and more complete humanity' (1922, p. 427). The current generation is the first to be able to bring the lifecourse to its natural fulfillment. For various reasons the time is propitious for a campaign to bring about a wisdom society.

The quickest and most effective path to creation of a wisdom society may be via the elderly. This is a group whose ability to complete a full lifecycle enables them to respond to the desire to leave a judiciously-chosen legacy, make sense of their lives, and develop the comprehensive understanding and character that is wisdom. Centers for learning in retirement may provide an ideal starting-point for this evolutionary step.

From what has been said about *Homo sapiens'* current attainment of wisdom, it is obvious that this paper is only an inchoative statement, leaving vital questions unraised. The biological basis of wisdom, gender differences, the ambiguities of human nature, productive approaches to conceptualizing the human condition, the organizing of priorities, the role of character and virtue in manifesting wisdom—and human limits in this regard—are some vexed questions awaiting future exploration. Also, understanding wisdom and optimal human development requires a multicultural approach going beyond the western focus presented here. Ways to include non-white, less formally educated and less financially secure people—who are poorly represented in learning in retirement institutions—need to be found. In the meantime, we can still go much farther than we have.

Notes on contributor

Richard Hawley Trowbridge teaches critical thinking and human relations courses for under-graduates, in addition to conducting courses in wisdom development for older people. He is currently completing a volume that integrates approaches to wisdom from philosophy, theology, and psychology, and proposes ways in which wisdom can be applied to contemporary problems of living.

References

American Association of Retired Persons (AARP) (2005) *Boomers at midlife: the AARP life stage study wave 3, 2004.* Available online at: http://assets.aarp.org/rgcenter/general/boomers_midlife_2004.pdf (accessed 26 January 2007).

Baltes, P. B. (1993) The aging mind: potential and limits, *The Gerontologist,* 33(5), 580–594.

Baltes, P. B. (2004) *Wisdom as orchestration of mind and virtue.* Book in preparation. Available online at: www.mpib-berlin.mpg.de/dok/full/baltes/orchestr/index.htm (accessed 26 January 2007).

Baltes, P. B. & Freund, A. M. (2003) The intermarriage of wisdom and selective optimization with compensation: two meta-heuristics guiding the conduct of life, in: C. L. M. Keyes & J. Haidt (Eds) *Flourishing: positive psychology and the life well-lived* (Washington, DC, American Psychology Association), 149–173.

Baltes, P. B., Freund, A. M. & Li, S.-C. (2005) The psychological science of human aging, in: M. L. Johnson (Ed.) *The Cambridge handbook of age and ageing* (Cambridge, Cambridge University Press), 47–71.

Baltes, P. B., Smith, J. & Staudinger, U. M. (1991) Wisdom and successful aging, in: T. Sonderegger (Ed.) *Nebraska symposium on motivation.* Volume 39 (Lincoln, NB, University of Nebraska Press), 123–167.

Baltes, P. B. & Staudinger, U. M. (2000) Wisdom: a metaheuristic (pragmatic) to orchestrate mind and virtue toward excellence, *American Psychologist*, 55(1), 122–136.

Beckett, C. (2002) *Human growth and development.* (London, Sage).

Birren, J. E. (1999) Theories of aging: a personal perspective, in: V. L. Bengtson & K. W. Schaie (Eds) *Handbook of theories of aging* (New York, Springer).

Clayton, V. (1975) Erikson's theory of human development as it applies to the aged: wisdom as contradictive cognition, *Human Development*, 18(1/2), 119–128.

Clayton, V. (1976) *A multidimensional scaling analysis of the concept of wisdom.* Unpublished dissertation, Los Angeles, CA, University of Southern California.

David, G. (2001) Aging, religion, and spirituality: advancing meaning in later life, in: F. L. Ahearn (Ed.) *Issues in global aging* (New York, Haworth Press), 129–140.

Dreyfus, H. L. & Dreyfus, S. E. (1986) *Mind over machine: the power of human intuition and expertise in the era of the computer* (New York, Free Press).

Dreyfus, H. L. & Dreyfus, S. E. (2004) From Socrates to expert systems: the limits and dangers of calculative rationality. Available online at: http://ist-socrates.berkeley.edu/~hdreyfus/html/paper_socrates.html (accessed 9 February 2006).

Elderhostel (2007) *Elderhostel Institute Network.* Available online at: http://www.elderhostel.org/ein/intro.asp (accessed 14 January 2007).

Erikson, E. H. (1950) *Childhood and society* (New York, Norton).

Erikson, E. H. (1963) *Childhood and society* (New York, Norton).

Erikson, E. H. (1997) *The life cycle completed* (New York, W. W. Norton).

Freud, S. (1935) *A general introduction to psycho-analysis* (New York, Liveright).

Friedan, B. (1993) *The fountain of age* (New York, Simon & Schuster).

Hadot, P. (2002) *What is ancient philosophy?* (Cambridge, MA, Belknap-Harvard University Press).

Hall, G. S. (1922) *Senescence, the last half of life* (New York, Appleton).

Havighurst, R. (1976) Education through the adult life span, *Educational Gerontology*, 1(1), 41–51.

Jung, C. G. (1969) The stages of life, in: *The collected works of C. G. Jung* (Bollingen Series XX), Vol. 8: *The structure and dynamics of the psyche* (Princeton, NJ, Princeton University Press).

Kim, A. & Merriam, S. B. (2004) Motivations for learning among older adults in a learning in retirement institute, *Educational Gerontology*, 30(6), 441–455.

Kinsella, K. & Velkoff, V. A. (2001) *An aging world: 2001*, US Census Bureau, Series P95/01-1 (Washington, DC, US Government Printing Office).

Kolata, G. (2006, July 30) So big and healthy grandpa wouldn't even know you, *New York Times.* Available online at: http://www.nytimes.com/2006/07/30/health/30age.html?ex=1182916800&en=9aa0441e9f0ad040&ei=5070 (accessed 12 June 2007).

Lamb, R. & Brady, E. M. (2005) Participation in lifelong learning institutes: what turns members on?, *Educational Gerontology*, 31(3), 207–224.

Londoner, C. A. (1978) Instrumental and expressive education: a basis for needs assessment and planning, in: R. H. Sherron & D. B. Lumsden (Eds) *Introduction to educational gerontology* (Washington, DC, Hemisphere).

Manheimer, R., Snodgrass, D. D. & Moskow-McKenzie, D. (1995) *Older adult education: a guide to research, programs, and policies* (Westport, CT, London, Greenwood Press).

Marcel, G. (1955) *The decline of wisdom* (New York, Philosophical Library).

Martin, C. (2003) Learning in retirement institutes: the impact on the lives of older adults, *Journal of Continuing Higher Education*, 51(1), 2–11.

Maslow, A. H. (1968) *Toward a psychology of being* (New York, Van Nostrand).

Maslow, A. H. (1969) The farther reaches of human nature, *Journal of Transpersonal Psychology*, 1(1), 1–9.

Maslow, A. H (1970) *Motivation and personality* (New York, Harper & Bros.).

Maslow, A.H. (1987) *Motivation and personality* (New York, Harper & Row).

Moody, H. R. 1978. Education and the life cycle: a philosophy of aging, in: R. H. Sherron, & D. B. Lumsden (Eds.) *Introduction to educational gerontology* (Washington, DC, Hemisphere), 31–47.

Moody, H. R. (2003) Conscious aging: a strategy for positive change in later life, in: J. L. Ronch & J. A. Goldfield (Eds) *Mental wellness in aging: strengths-based approaches* (Baltimore, MD, Health Professions Press), 139–160.

Office of National Statistics (2001) *Table KS02 Age structure, census 2001: key statistics for the rural and urban area classification 2004.* Available online at: www.statistics.gov.uk/StatBase/Expodata/Spreadsheets/D8915.xls (accessed 26 January 2007).

Olson, E. (2006, October 24) Community colleges want you, *New York Times.* Available online at: http://www.nytimes.com/2006/10/24/business/retirement/24educ.html?ex=1319342400&en=d541ee2a2c8202cd&ei=5088&partner=rssnyt&emc=rss (accessed 12 June 2007).

Pascual-Leone, J. (1990) An essay on wisdom: toward organismic processes that make it possible, in: R. Sternberg (Ed.) *Wisdom* (Cambridge, Cambridge University Press), 244–278.

Piaget, J. (1932) *The moral development of the child* (New York, Harcourt, Brace & World).

Piaget, J. (1966) *The psychology of intelligence* (Totowa, NJ, Littlefield, Adams & Co).

Rowe, J. W. & Kahn, R. L. (1998) *Successful aging* (New York, Pantheon).

Ryff, C. D. & Singer, B. (1998) The contours of positive human health, *Psychological Inquiry,* 9(1), 1–28.

Sinnott, J. D. (1998) Creativity and postformal thought: why the last stage is the creative stage, in: C. E. Adams-Price (Ed.) *Creativity and successful aging: theoretical and empirical approaches* (New York, Springer), 43–72.

Smith, N. D. (1998) Wisdom, in: E. Craig (General Ed.) *Routledge encyclopedia of philosophy* (London, Routledge), 752–755.

Staudinger, U. (1999) Older and wiser? Integrating results on the relationship between age and wisdom-related performance, *International Journal of Behavioral Development,* 23(3), 641–664.

Taylor, R. (2005) Lifelong learning and the Labour governments 1997–2004, *Oxford Review of Education,* 31(1), 101–118.

Tornstam, L. (1997) Gero-transcendence: the contemplative dimension of aging, *Journal of Aging Studies,* 11(2), 143–154.

Trowbridge, R. H. (2005) *The scientific approach to wisdom.* Unpublished doctoral dissertation. Available online at: www.cop.com/TheScientificApproachtoWisdom.doc (accessed 26 January 2007).

University of the Third Age/Third Age Trust (2007) Home page. Available online at: www.u3a-info.co.uk (accessed 14 January 2007).

Vaillant, G. E. (2002) *Aging well: surprising guideposts to a happier life from the landmark Harvard study of adult development* (Boston, MA, Little, Brown & Company).

Withnall, A. (2000) *Older learners—issues and perspectives. Working papers of the Global Colloquium on Supporting Lifelong Learning.* Available online at: www.open.ac.uk/lifelong-learning (accessed 12 December 2006).

World Health Organization (1948) Preamble to the constitution of the World Health Organization as adopted by the International Health Conference, New York, 19–22 June, 1946; signed on 22 July 1946 by the representatives of 61 States (Official Records of the World Health Organization, no. 2, p. 100) and entered into force on 7 April 1948.

Wisdom remembered: recovering a theological vision of wisdom *for* the academe

Celia Deane-Drummond

Introduction

Consider one of the most contested issues for public debate in recent years, namely, the genetic modification of foods. When social scientists first engaged with this problem they largely ignored the possibility that religious questions and issues might be relevant. For example, social scientists working at Lancaster University interviewed a number of different groups in order to glean what might be motivating public interest. The published report—entitled *Uncertain world*—contained virtually no reference to religion (Grove-White *et al.*, 1999). When these same transcripts received greater scrutiny some time later, it soon became clear that implicit religious issues were highly significant in shaping public opinion (this was published in Deane-Drummond *et al.*, 2001, and in Deane-Drummond &

Szerszynski, 2003). This short story illustrates a number of issues. In the first place, the fact that religion was ignored in the first instance shows that religious issues have become marginal to the thinking of many serious academics. As a subject discipline, where religious studies is accepted at a university, it tends to ape other areas of science, and be treated methodologically in the same sort of way as a detached academic discipline in order to give it greater credibility in the academe. Theology is even more the Cinderella subject, often appearing as a laughing stock to other academics as illustrated in David Lodges's popular but fictional University of Rummage (Lodge, 1991). This is a far cry from theology's role as 'queen of the sciences' in the thirteenth century. A second point, however, is that even in Britain, arguably a largely secular society, the public have not forgotten the long history of religious experience that is embedded in their consciousness. This is often not necessarily explicit religious practice, but it surfaces in the recognition of the importance of religious concerns for informing the way we live, however far they may be from traditional theological formulations. I suggest that attempts to suppress this wisdom comes about, at least in part, from the captivity of universities to the Enlightenment agenda that has served simply to reinforce a utilitarian means for education.

In fact, in order to survive, theology has been forced to capitulate to the academic agenda dictated by its secular partners. Students are now asked to make sense of scripture, instead of scripture making sense of them. Theology becomes 'domesticated and secularized', most important of all, theology is prized apart from praxis, so that skills learnt in theology are now named as 'transferable skills' (D'Costa, 2002, pp. 186, 189). Those engaged in religious studies take this detachment still further, so that students are encouraged to keep an entirely neutral stance towards religions, combined with objectivity and Enlightenment reasoning. But, say the critics, surely such neutrality is essential to foster mutual respect and understanding in this world of divided religious sensibilities and religious fundamentalisms? Some even suggest that any idea of promoting the possibility of a Christian University is paramount to a perversion of the true intention of a university, namely to encourage free thought. The assumption in this case, is that tradition of any kind is inimical to free enquiry (Thiessen, 2002). Indeed, the search for truth as evidenced in the modern university is one dogged by the legacy of the Enlightenment and a utilitarian attitude to knowledge, reflected in methodologies that are there to provide rules and systems of analysis, but are thereby constricting in their perception of epistemology. Consider, for example, the increasing interest across different universities in providing courses in empirical methodologies for doctoral students, as if all theses need to be squeezed into appropriately sanctioned methodologies even before they emerge.

John Henry Newman's vision for higher education

The seeds for much of the developments we see today have a long history, and were apparent to Cardinal John Henry Newman, writing in the middle of the nineteenth century, at just about the same time as when Charles Darwin was penning his *Origin of species*, a work whose influence continues to reverberate even outside the discipline of biology. John Newman's work is less well known and appreciated by the public. He lived at a time when individualism was coming to the fore, and epistemic narrowness and simplicity replaced former, broader ways of thinking (for a discussion of his work see Robinson (2002). The dramatic advances in science that began in the seventeenth century were beginning to be felt in the public domain, and alongside this an aping of the epistemology of science throughout the university environment, that is, the Academe. Newman recognized there was some worth in scientific knowing, that he described in terms of *notional* apprehension, that is, apprehension that is deductive, scientific and logically conclusive. However, he also argued for *real* apprehension, that is, knowing from a variety of factors through a collection of what he terms weak evidences. These included notions, images, historical occurrences, and emotions. The illative sense constructs knowledge through practice, so that there is a 'going round an object, by the comparison, the combination, the mutual correction, the continual adaptation of many partial notions, by the employment, concentration and joint action of many faculties and exercises of the mind' (Newman, 1852). Hence, for real apprehension there needs to be a greater sensitivity to the complexity of truth, for the world is also complex. Newman believed that if we oversimplify we fail in imagination, for we are not recognizing the truth that emerges out of daily activity.

The essence of ideology and indeed for him, heresy, is a failure to see tensions embedded in truths that are not necessarily resolvable. Such a view also echoes the thoughts of modern contemporary theologians, such as Nicholas Lash, who claims that univocal thinking such as that portrayed in much science, has effectively shut out other imaginative ways of knowing (Lash, 1996). Newman also compared education to the nature of divine reality, so that the more one knows, the more one realizes that one does not know. Such a way of knowing that is also informed by practices means that it can be of service to the public good because it is influenced by a more rounded approach to truth. Newman believed that the only authentic university is also Christian because he believed that knowledge of God was necessary for complete learning. This is a different way of reasoning compared with that common among utilitarians, that views learning as only useful if it is practical. The idea that knowledge of the natural world could be gained through construction became dominant over more contemplative forms of knowing that had been the case in earlier centuries (see Funkenstein, 1986, p. 12, 297ff.). Here the knowledge base is monocular. Instead, for Newman, the task of a university is purposefully to complicate the process by introducing convolution of learning that belies simple conveyance of information and techné (Robinson, 2002, p. 89). Universities are, instead, to become in this way, 'seats of wisdom', such that they encourage a multidimensional approach.[1] Indeed, according to this model, interdisciplinary study is not simply a good idea or a particular educational philosophy but essential in order to promote a well-rounded student.

More important, perhaps, for Newman education is not just a passive reception of knowledge, but a way of life, so that 'universities inspire learners not to knowledge as a goal, but to the wisdom that a life of learning instils' (Robinson, 2002, p. 93). He also believed that knowledge ceases to be knowledge in so far as it tends more and more to the particular. How different from the fragmentation in departments across universities with their urge to ever greater specialization as a way of attracting greater recognition of the 'expert', itself showing a limited understanding, especially in the public sphere (see comment of this aspect in Deane-Drummond et al., 2001, pp. 24–25). For Newman, university life needs to be more conscious and rely on close cooperation between people, for it needs to reflect the collected wisdom of those from different subject areas, experiences and levels of education.

Why might we need theological wisdom?

If, according to Newman, God is the fount of wisdom, what might this mean? Biblical scholars have become more focused on the wisdom literature, reflecting neglect in earlier scholarship. The question that concerns us here is, in what way might the tradition of theological wisdom serve to inform the ethos of higher education? I suggest that wisdom does have something useful to say in debates about the role of the university today. In the first place, theological wisdom draws on education in the context of family and community. This way of learning was *practical* and *contextual* long before theologies bearing such a name came to the fore, largely in reaction to more theoretical doctrinal discussions about God that seemed far too detached from ordinary life. This *praxis* or theory informed by practices, is very different from utilitarian methods that simply emphasize usefulness for its own sake and as a means of control, detached from other forms of knowing and contemplation. If we apply this to the university, then the context of students' living and community life is just as important as what they learn, a point that the university where I teach is keen to make, for smaller institutions are able to achieve this sense of community more easily than the mega-universities that have grown up from mergers of smaller institutions, supposedly to succeed in becoming 'world class' institutions of learning.

Secondly, theological wisdom is expressed in the Hebrew Bible in feminine categories.[2] Christian theology has been dogged in its history by interpretations of theology that are influenced by patriarchal societies and assumptions. Catherine Keller, a leading feminist theologian, has drawn on the idea of *emancipatory wisdom* as that which best describes the future of theology in the university (Keller, 1991). It is wisdom that can straddle the world of the academic and ecclesial communities to which theology must give an account of itself. For Keller, wisdom 'at least as practised in the indigenous and biblical traditions, is irredeemably implicated in the sensuous, the communal, the experiential, the metanoic, the unpredictable, the imaginal, the practical' (Keller, 1991, p. 143).[3] This differs significantly from the coercive control of matter by mind, which is the agenda of modernity. Rather, it takes time to 'let things become' and includes the social and well as the cosmological. Theological wisdom, therefore, is not individualistic, but operates from within the social context, and reaches out more widely than this to the natural world as well. It has the capacity, therefore, of enlarging a person's horizons to think of those issues that are important not just to the human community, but to the community of others in the world that God has created. Indeed, based on reflections on Proverbs 8, God could be said to create the world in love, but through wisdom.[4] Hence wisdom is a fundamental characteristic of the way God is perceived to create and sustain the world, perceived as a child at play, ever present with God at the dawn of existence. Yet such a theological interpretation of creation in wisdom is not at loggerheads with cosmological and evolutionary accounts of the origin of the earth (Deane-Drummond, 2006b). Rather, it adds to such an account a dimension that fills out an interpretation of human origins in a way that complements the voice of science.

Thirdly, a theological voice is one that needs to be heard, for without it more extreme voices start to force their way into education's agenda. Such a worrying trend is only too apparent in the way that those wishing to promote creationism, the belief that the story of Genesis is literally true and an alternative to the evolutionary account of science, has begun to creep its way into the school curriculum in the UK. While creationist science's voice has become rather more sophisticated through the notion of Intelligent Design, it still seeks to provide through ideology an alternative to Darwinian notions of evolutionary science. It is hardly surprising that, given this trend, virtually all universities in the US wish to keep theology out of their agenda. Yet, perhaps it is for this reason that such counter-reactions have found their force? For if people are inculcated into utilitarian methods of learning and thinking at universities, then a culture that is generally religious will sense some disorientation and so be more inclined to an equally narrow reaction to that utilitarianism. In other words, a narrowing of epistemology through a secularist agenda as that expressed in university education leads to a counter reaction that is ironically a very reflection of such narrowness, but this time it is expressed in religious terms. Hence, the importance of a rich understanding of theological wisdom that will discourage such retreats into apparently safe havens, excluded from the worst excesses of those particular forms of scientific knowing that then subsequently become expressed in narrow public policies and practices.

Fourthly, and more radical perhaps, the New Testament theological wisdom finds expression through paradox of suffering, rather than a celebration of human wisdom, in the wisdom of the cross.[5] While not doing away with the wisdom of the sages, the wisdom of the cross points to another way of being that makes most sense in the context of the Christian community. Yet could the wisdom of the cross also have wider relevance as well? Certainly, it shows that a Christian image of God is one that is on the side of those who are suffering and in pain. One of the important tasks of the university is pastoral; students do not achieve in a vacuum, but are enabled through their lived experiences. If such experiences are too traumatic, learning may suffer, at least temporarily. It is here that a university needs to include not just a curricula programme, but also provide for pastoral needs of its students through adequate counseling and Chaplaincy provision. Discussions of the wisdom of the cross in the epistle to the Corinthians are also set in the context of an early Christian community where different groups were vying for authority according to different perceptions of wisdom. Instead of such rhetorical game playing, the author of the epistle encourages reflection on the wisdom of the cross. Such wisdom speaks, of the need for humility, rather than jockeying for positions of power through clever forms of speech. Is such a goal realistic in a university context? What would the shape of university management be like if such an approach was adopted by vice chancellors? I suggest that the cooperation indicated as necessary in the previous section presupposes this form of wisdom to some extent, for without mutual respect and understanding will fail to emerge.

Why might we need practical wisdom?

The medieval theologian Thomas Aquinas distinguished between the intellectual virtues of speculative reason and those of practical reason. The intellectual virtues of speculative reason included understanding, science, and wisdom, where wisdom is the appreciation of the fundamental causes of everything and the connections between them, including God. The practical virtues, on the other hand, included art and prudence, or practical wisdom.[6] Prudence in the classical sense, includes deliberation, judgement and action. How might prudence inform institutions such as a university? First, prudence is both individual and political. Hence, it has a social dimension as well, so that there is a need not just to encourage students to think prudentially, but also apply this to forms of management and institutional structures as well. Yet prudence in a popular cast of mind is often portrayed as caution about taking risks, at least as applied to political decision making. The classical notion is so different that it is worth considering whether the term prudence should still be used in such a context. I suggest that it can, as long as appropriate care is taken to explain what prudence might be.

Prudence, for the classics, has a number of different facets that are worth highlighting in this context. In the first place, it is sensitive to memory of the past, that is, it is conscious of the history of what has gone before and learnt the lessons from this history. John Henry Newman's approach to university education has been largely ignored, at least in terms of practical application. It is time, therefore, to propose an alternative style of university ethos compared with the current focus on utilitarian management so that universities are enabled to become, as Newman suggested, 'seats of wisdom'. Alasdair MacIntyre argued in this vein when he suggested that there are three rival versions of moral inquiry, only one of which has served to inform the modern university, namely the one based on the Enlightenment project of liberal modernity (MacIntyre, 1990). The second tradition that he identifies is what he terms the geneology of Nietzsche, which leads to forms of postmodernity that seek to deconstruct all foundations for knowledge. If such a postmodern project were taken too literally, then it is hard to imagine how universities might function.[7] The third form of inquiry that he identifies is that of Thomas Aquinas, that he suggests provides a bridge between universal forms of disembodied reason found in the first Enlightenment project, and the second form that encourages relativism. Certainly, the Aristotelian tradition of prudence influences that of Aquinas, but I suggest that Aquinas's view goes even further than just providing a bridge between modern and postmodern views in the way that MacIntyre suggests. For Aquinas holds fast to the importance of theology in his construction; it is not simply an 'add on', in the manner of grace being added to nature in the way he is sometimes portrayed in basic textbooks in theology. Rather, Aquinas, is sensitive to the importance of religious experience, even admitting towards the end of his life that he had not given sufficient attention to such experience in his great *Summa Theologiae*. There is, in other words, in Aquinas a sensitivity to the presence of God, a contemplative dimension, that MacIntyre has not taken sufficiently seriously. Prudence for Aquinas is not simply learnt in the human community; it is also a gift of the Holy Spirit received by the grace of God. In addition, for Aquinas, prudence, along with the other cardinal virtues, also presuppose the theological virtues of faith, hope and charity.

Secondly, practical wisdom in Aquinas is conscious of what is the case in the present, and is open to being taught. This openness is an essential ingredient of all learning, whatever level and whatever the final goal of such learning. Deliberation needs to include, therefore, consultation with others, both within and outside the discipline to which individuals belong. Furthermore, are such disciplines open to being restructured? Theology, that Gavin D'Costa has described as being 'in Babylonian captivity' by its aping of secular agendas, could arguably be the first to remember its lost wisdom and seek alternatives (D'Costa, 2002). While other disciplines might find it hard to extricate themselves from the specialism that seems to engender authority and funding, at least as a first move different subject areas could seek to scrutinize the overall goals of their research and knowledge transfer programmes. Practical wisdom is also able to make correct decisions in the face of the unexpected. If universities are to become those seats of wisdom, then they too will have something to say when unexpected events happen that need public comment, as discussed in more detail in the final section below.

Thirdly, practical wisdom combines both caution, and also foresight. Caution is awareness of where mistakes have been made in the past, and being able to adjust future policy in the light of those mistakes. Have universities really learnt from their mistakes, or are they bent on ever more accumulative strategies that are orientated to utilitarian goals? Can foresight enable universities to see into the future as to what different strategies might entail, and how each might be implemented? If universities continue to be led by market driven policies, then not only will the basis for learning be undermined, for some subjects will disappear as being unfashionable, but also universities will become narrowed to centres for vocational training, the curriculum adjusted to what is needed for a market economy. In this way, the university is no longer a place where new questions are asked of society, but one where values in society are simply reinforced.

What might an alternative vision include? In Aquinas, practical wisdom is wisdom orientated towards the good. Although there are philosophical debates about what this good might entail, a vision for the public good, that is, the good for the whole community, goes some way towards expressing what he intends. A Christian university would also wish this good to be grounded in an understanding of theological good, for Aquinas this Divine Wisdom is reflected in practical terms through the Decalogue, that is, The Ten Commandments. Although detached from its origins, the legal structure that exists in Britain is also influenced by the Christian context in which it emerged. Yet universities need to seek not just to encourage its students to be law-abiding citizens, though certainly they can do this, but might also seek to serve the communities in which they are placed.

Practical wisdom in service to the public good

In order to illustrate how practical wisdom might inform the public good I am going to use two different areas of public discussion, namely, environmental concerns and the new reproductive technologies. Both areas are subjects of considerable contested public debate. What might a prudential approach, understood according to the classical tradition that I have been elaborating, have to say on these issues? While it is quite possible to understand prudence without any reference to Christian theology, I suggest that retrieving a classical and Thomistic notion of prudence that acknowledges its links with Christian virtue serves to provide a bridge between secular and religious aspects of human community that also help serve the public good. In other words, we do not just need a bridge between modern and postmodern, that MacIntyre correctly identifies as one of the roles of virtue traditions, but also a bridge between secular and religious streams of human life.

This essay need hardly convince its readers that environmental issues are important. Nearly every day some topic is discussed in the media, the issue of climate change has somewhat surprisingly surfaced comparatively late in terms of media reporting, and popular wildlife programmes have engendered greater sensitivity to the importance of thinking holistically about our planet and its future. The language that has begun to dominate the discussion of environmental responsibility is that of sustainability. Sustainability is a subject that lends itself to a multidisciplinary approach, from geography, through to social science, anthropology and theology. It is, also, subject to captivity to the market in common with other ways of thinking, in that it can become a market commodity that merely serves to promote economic interests. It also allows for a theological dimension for a number of reasons.

In the first place, the religious aspects to sustainability processes are often thought of by practical campaign groups as simply there to reinforce a sustainable agenda. If Christians are able to support sustainability because of their faith commitment, then, the argument goes, so much the better, for religious motivation will reinforce commitment. Yet, in consultations on what sustainability might mean, which often includes an account of future generations, little account has been taken of what Christian communities might have to say on sustainability and what sustainability might or needs to include.[8] This exclusion of Christian communities as having something worthwhile to say reflects, it seems to me, a lack of prudence or practical wisdom, for it narrows thinking accordingly to a materialistic agenda.

The Revd. John Rodwell is seeking to correct this anomaly by research that deliberately interrelates social, economic and environmental patterns alongside patterns of church activity. As a former professor of ecology he brings to the subject both experience of practical ecology alongside experience as a Christian minister. He has also investigated the way particular environmental groups in a given area understand sustainability. The need for specific measurable targets for sustainability that could be demonstrated and assessed in groups such as RSPB is one that is largely controlled by Government funding which seeks particular performance indicators. This example illustrates that the public good in the area of sustainability is one that is narrowed to information gathering, reflecting an equally pervasive narrowness that characterizes universities. Hence, if universities are to demonstrate that practical wisdom that I have argued is necessary in order to expand notions of the good, then there needs to be wider political scrutiny not just of what sustainability might mean and how it is defined, but also how it is practised in given environmental organizations as well.

In addition, environments that are sustainable need to be places where we feel at home, engendering connectivity with the past. Does sustainability in its current definitions take into account this need for *memory*, which is also another vital aspect of prudential reasoning? Rodwell questions whether 'the sustainability process knows how to handle the past at all' (Rodwell, 2006). There is, furthermore, a lack of appreciation in visions of a sustainable future as to whether justice has been done to the past, for the focus is on the needs of future generations, or that of the more immediate ecological community.

A second example that is worth noting in this context is that of new reproductive technologies (for a detailed discussion of the application of prudence to discussions about genetics see Deane-Drummond, 2006a). One reason for this is that while Christian views may be excluded from public debates about environmental questions, or perhaps only aired in Christian communities, religious attitudes to new reproductive technologies are more often than not aired in public. One of the reasons for this difference may be that Christian reflection is not perceived as having something of interest to say on the matter of the environment, even though this is a misconception, as illustrated above. Secondly, the very public feuds over human dignity and religious passions surrounding this issue generate stories that the media like to portray, for it leads to two different rhetorical strategies focused on the embryo as personal or as a pinprick ball of cells that make for good broadcasting (for a discussion of this aspect see Kitzinger & Williams, 2006). Yet, just as in the above account, the portrayal of religious views as equated with conservative ethics, more often than not pitched against the new reproductive technologies, is far too simplistic. In the first place, practical wisdom would encourage a more holistic understanding of issues that takes into account different facets of knowledge, rather than tying religion to a specific conservative ethic in the manner of media debate. In the second place, prudential reflection would seek to engage with the overall goal of the technologies themselves, and ask social justice questions that are broader than questions simply about the moral status of the embryo. Thirdly, prudence is a stance that encourages some flexibility in approach to new reproductive technologies, even though the boundaries of what is acceptable may be defined through particular principles.

A good example of this is the current discussion on the use of chimeras in order to generate embryonic stem cells. For scientists, this alleviates the need to find women who are prepared to be donors, with the associated risks that this entails. The relaxation in the law that allows donors to offer their eggs for research, with generous 'compensation' payable, rather than their use in the fertility treatment of themselves or others, also increases availability of eggs. In this case it treats eggs more like commodities that can be bought and sold in a manner that would not be acceptable for other body parts. It is therefore not surprising that many theologians are suspicious of the new technologies and their futures, not just because they seem to be an affront to embryos, but also because of the underlying control over life and the drive towards perfectibility that this implies (for discussion of a range of different theological standpoints see Deane-Drummond, 2003; Deane-Drummond & Scott, 2006).

Debates exist as to how far and to what extent technological intervention is desirable or acceptable. While some theologians warm to the possibility of technological change, and celebrate advances in medicine, viewing such human capacities as representing humanity as co-creators, others are more wary. In the latter case theologians believe that human life in particular should be treated as gift, where chance as an element in the formation of life is respected, and where sexuality is not separated from human reproduction. Clearly, universities need to involve themselves in debates such as these, by hosting public forums, for example, in such a way that public debate is informed by accurate representation of all facets of the topic, both from the medical, social, philosophical, ethical, historical and theological perspectives.

Conclusions

I suggest that a religious dimension to public debate is forgotten at its peril. Universities are also subject to this same form of forgetting. I have argued that we can learn some important lessons about the possible shape of university education by returning to the work of John Henry Newman. He lived at a time when knowledge was becoming ever more narrow in its focus, excluding what once had been presupposed as a good. His concept of a Christian University is not simply an argument for permission of existence of such institutions. Rather, I suggest that his thinking has wider application, and can contribute to the construction of an overall shape for university education. Not all universities will have the same agenda, but all can be challenged to encourage in their students more holistic ways of learning. This includes a seeking of wisdom that is multidimensional in its scope.

I have also argued that theological wisdom is important in that it has become a voice that is often marginalized and excluded from university educational agendas. Yet this very exclusion is a mistake, for within theology there are resources that can make a valuable contribution to re-envisioning an agenda for higher education. In particular, this agenda needs to be emancipatory, but such emancipatory knowing is one that is practical, and well as multifaceted.

Newman's vision of cooperation comes to the fore here, for without mutual respect for the contribution of different disciplines, soon universities start to imitate that divided community of Corinth where each group vied for its own superiority.[9] Instead, proper account needs to be made of the common good, and how to reach this goal in the context of the local and wider community.

Thomas Aquinas' brilliance in synthesizing the thought of Aristotle with Augustine still has relevance today, especially in his discussion of practical wisdom or prudence. universities too need to be places where synthetic knowledge is encouraged, especially if they are to form seeds for alternative ways of thinking that resist monocular thinking.

Public debates are too often ill informed not only about science, which is perhaps recognized, but also about the place of religious understanding, as illustrated from discussions of sustainability and new reproductive technologies. Universities need, therefore, to be places that can inform public opinion so that more accurate representation takes place. In this way, a public that is better informed than would otherwise be the case will serve to help shape Government policy.

Moreover, universities need to be places that instill in those who study there the love of learning that goes far deeper than simple success at examinations. For the kind of wisdom that is instilled offers skills that are not just 'transferable', but help to foster *citizen virtues*, those who are able to take active and full responsibility not just in their family life, but in the public sphere as well.

Notes

1. Newman did recognize that some universities would be specialist, but he argued that the ideal of universality should prevail, rather than some subjects being excluded as a matter of principle.
2. I am confining my discussion of wisdom to Christian theology, but this should not be taken to imply that I think that other religions have little to offer debates on wisdom.
3. Note that metanoic has meaning here of being capable of changing hearts, from *metanoia,* change of heart.
4. A full discussion of this is outside the scope of this chapter. For more detail see Deane-Drummond (2000).
5. The first letter of Paul to the Corinthians, for example, especially I Cor. 1.8–2.5.
6. Aquinas distinguished wisdom, a virtue of speculative reason, from prudence, a virtue of practical reason, by naming wisdom as that which dealt specifically with theological matters, and prudence as that which dealt with human affairs. For his discussion of wisdom see Aquinas, *Summa Theologiae,* volume 34 (1975, 2a2ae). For his discussion of prudence see Aquinas, *Summa Theologiae,* volume 36 (1973).
7. A caveat for this view is that arguably Derrida's own view of endless questioning means that the University is still obliged to remember the older universal story in its questioning, rather than simply cast this to one side. See Loughlin (20002).
8. I am drawing here on the work of Rev. Professor John Rodwell and his M.B. Reckitt Lecture, 'Forgetting the Land', delivered at Mirfield College, 7 September 2006.
9. I am referring here to the portrayal of this community by the apostle Paul in his first letter to the Corinthians.

Notes on contributor

Celia Deane-Drummond is Professor of Theology and the Biological Sciences at the University of Chester and Director of the Centre for Religion and the Biosciences, which was founded in 2002. She has published widely on the theme of wisdom, including for example, *Creation through Wisdom: Theology and the New Biology,* T & T Clark, 2000.

References

Aquinas (1973) *Summa Theologiae. Volume 36, Prudence* (London, Blackfriars).

Aquinas (1975) *Summa Theologiae. Volume 34, Charity* (London, Blackfriars).

Astley, J., Francis, L., Sullivan, J. & Walker, A. (2004) *The idea of a Christian university: essays in theology and higher education* (Carlisle, Paternoster Press).

D'Costa, G. (2002) On theology's Babylonian captivity within the secular university, in: J. Astley, L. Francis, J. Sullivan & A. Walker (Eds) *The idea of a Christian university: essays in theology and higher education* (Carlisle, Paternoster Press), 183–199.

Deane-Drummond, C. (2000) *Creation through wisdom: theology and the new biology* (Edinburgh, T & T Clark).

Deane-Drummond, C. (2003) *Brave new world: theology, ethics and the human genome* (London, Continuum).

Deane-Drummond, C. (2006a) *Genetics and Christian ethics* (Cambridge, Cambridge University Press).

Deane-Drummond, C. (2006b) *Wonder and wisdom: conversations in science, spirituality and theology* (London, DLT).

Deane-Drummond C. & Scott, P. (2006) *Future perfect: god, medicine and human identity* (London, Continuum).

Deane-Drummond, C., Grove-White, R. & Szerszynski, B. (2001) Genetically modified theology: the religious dimensions of public concerns about agricultural biotechnology, *Studies in Christian Ethics,* 14(2), 23–41.

Funkenstein, A. (1986) *Theology and the scientific imagination* (Princeton, Princeton University Press).

Grove-White, R., Macnaghten, P., Mayer, S. & Wynne, B. (1999) *Uncertain world: genetically modified organisms, food and public attitudes in Britain* (Lancaster, Centre for the Study of Environmental Change, Lancaster University).

Keller, C. (1991) Towards an emancipatory wisdom, in: D. R. Griffin & J. C. Hough (Eds) *Theology and the university: essays in honour of John B. Cobb, Jr* (Albany, State University of New York Press), 125–147.

Kitzinger, J. & Williams, C. (2006) Forecasting the future: legitimising hope and calming fears in the embryo stem cell debate, in: C. Deane-Drummond & P. Scott (Eds) *Future perfect: god, medicine and human identity* (London, Continuum), 129–142.

Lash, N. (1996) *The beginning and the end of religion* (Cambridge, Cambridge University Press).

Lodge, D. (1991) *Paradise news* (London, Secker & Warburg).

Loughlin, G. (2002) The university without question: John Henry Newman and Jacques Derrida on faith in the university, in: J. Astley, L. Francis, J. Sullivan & A. Walker (Eds) *The idea of a Christian university: essays in theology and higher education* (Carlisle, Paternoster Press), 113–131.

MacIntyre, A. (1990) *Three rival versions of moral enquiry* (London, Duckworth).

Newman, J. (1852) *The idea of the university* (London, Longmans, Green & Co).

Robinson, D. (2002) *Sedes Sapientiae*: Newman, truth and the christian Univerity, in: J. Astley, L. Francis, J. Sullivan & A. Walker (Eds) *The idea of a Christian university: essays in theology and higher education* (Carlisle, Paternoster Press), 75–97.

Rodwell, J. (2006) Forgetting the Land, M. B. Reckitt lecture, delivered at Mirfield College, 7 September.

Thiessen, J. H. (2002) Objections to the idea of a Christian university, in: J. Astley, L. Francis, J. Sullivan & A. Walker (Eds) *The idea of a Christian university: essays in theology and higher education* (Carlisle, Paternoster Press), 35–55.

Shakespeare on wisdom

Alan Nordstrom

In universities and elsewhere, might we study Shakespeare to learn about wisdom and how to grow wiser? I say yes, though in the language of one of Shakespeare's greatest fools:

> And thus do we of wisdom and of reach,
> With windlasses and with assays of bias
> By indirections find directions out. (HAM 2.1.63). [1]

Although Polonius' 'wisdom' here amounts merely to devious cunning, he nonetheless indicates Shakespeare's own way of revealing wisdom to us: indirectly, by showing us on his 'great stage of fools' (LR 4.6.183) so much of folly. While Erasmus wrote earlier *The praise of folly* and Burton later *The anatomy of melancholy*, Shakespeare's work falls between them as virtually *The anatomy of folly*, from which ironically we may infer something of what wisdom is and why it is so rare. Since Shakespeare is not an essayist but a playwright, he does not tell but show, thus we must learn not by precept but by instance and example. Examples of folly and error predominate in his plays, as they do in life as we know it, yet occasional sparks of wisdom shine out against the general gloom of human inanity and insanity.

Assuming with Nicholas Maxwell that wisdom is 'the capacity to realize what is of value in life, for oneself and others' (p. 98, this issue) (understanding 'realize' as both *comprehend* and *bring about*), then we may see why wisdom is so hard to come by. Too little do we know what's good for us or others or how to make it happen, which makes us fools, as Shakespeare knew long since. Add to that the innate perversity St Paul saw in us, which even when it knows what's good to do refuses to perform it. Or, in Portia's wry words to Nerissa: 'If to do were as easy as to know what were good to do, chapels had been churches, and poor men's cottages princes' palaces' (MV 1.2.12). The testimony is long and strong that being wise goes against our grain, and that even if we can agree that this or that decision produces the most value, we may still fail to execute it well and faithfully. In this skeptical light, I shall consider Shakespeare's take on human wisdom and our poor prospects of achieving it. Though I wish things otherwise and hope for better, I still must register this long-respected 'wisdom' of our master bard in finding us committed more to folly than its opposite. About human folly there's much to learn from Shakespeare, play after play, for, as Puck declares, 'Lord, what fools these mortals be!' (MND 3.2.115). But what about wisdom, folly's opposite—does Shakespeare show us that and give us any clues about living wisely?

Though he's never didactic, can we nonetheless deduce from his writing whether we mortals have any hope of escaping our innate proclivity to foolish error and of following a path toward wisdom? I think so, if only in flashes and glimpses easily missed by those with no eyes to see nor ears to hear. In each of his plays elements of wisdom may be detected, often ironically in those characters who appear most foolish—his motley fools and jesters—sometimes in simple and lowly characters, now and then in pure-hearted paragons, and more complexly in shrewd, intelligent, and insightful ones (presumably most like Shakespeare himself), whose wisdom is hard won and imperfect, and therefore more admirable and inspiring.

First, be clear: wisdom for Shakespeare has far more to do with the heart than the head. Though it is prudent to be canny and not gullible, and it is astute to be alert to the dangerous ways of the world (the flesh, and the devil), what is still more essential is a true and faithful heart, radiant with love, care and devotion, brimming with compassion and forgiveness. Those among Shakespeare's characters who are most bright, clever and cunning (such as Bolingbroke, Iago, Edmund, and to a degree Jaques and Puck) are typically bereft of fellow feeling, devoid of generosity, and radically unnatural in their unkindness (since kinship is the essence of nature). Therefore, when we search out wisdom in Shakespeare's plays, we seek not for hard heads so much as soft hearts, though preferably both—those qualities best exemplified in Viola, Rosalind, Desdemona, Cordelia, Kent, and incipiently in Prince Hal.

Shakespeare awake

> The breeze at dawn has secrets to tell you.
>> Don't go back to sleep.
> You must ask for what you really want.
>> Don't go back to sleep.
> People are going back and forth across the doorsill
>> where the two worlds touch.
> The door is round and open.
>> Don't go back to sleep.

(Jalal al-Din Rumi, p. 36)

Shakespeare fathomed our normal human penchant to sleepwalk through our lives, to stumble about in a fogbound world of dreams and delusions, oblivious of that grander reality accessible only to awakened consciousness. His plays mostly portray human beings in our typically benighted state of semi-consciousness, committing the common errors of blind waywardness and suffering the consequences, sometimes comic, sometimes tragic, of our befuddled foolishness. Our folly was his business. 'Lord, what fools these mortals be' might well have been a motto hung over his writing table.

The irony implicit in all his work, and what in part makes it immortal, is that Shakespeare was himself awake and wrote from a perspective that both mocked and lamented the follies he depicted. If the Buddha, the Awakened One, had been a dramatist, his plays might have been like Shakespeare's plays, revelations to those with eyes to see and ears to hear of the stumbling pageant of human error—our fickleness, inconstancy, mutability, and treachery. We are would-be angels who descend to bestiality. Yet Shakespeare was one who could not only write like an angel but see like one. His perspective is one of higher awareness, expanded consciousness, the viewpoint of seers and sages illumined by a transcendental gnosis that visionary mystics share. To see the world of mortal turmoil not from a dull sublunary vantage point is to see things steadily and see them whole, as Shakespeare quintessentially did.

Even we who have not his eyes and clarity of mind may still catch glimpses of the profundity of his insights as we experience his plays. If we cannot fully grasp the wisdom he possesses, we can better recognize our own folly by his fools and learn to laugh at it or mourn the miseries it brings. We may grow wiser by observing the spectacle he displays of dull Othello, obtuse Macbeth, perplexed Prince Hamlet, and love-blind King Lear. We may catch something of ourselves in asinine Bottom, mad-brained Mercutio, wild Kate, daft Orlando, buffoonish Falstaff and protean Cleopatra, among so many other characters uniquely stamped and stained: Beatrice and Benedick, Shylock, Iago, Brutus, crook-backed Richard, melancholy Jacques, primordial Caliban, and Juliet's garrulous nurse. They constitute a full catalogue of fools, a motley menagerie of lunatics and dunces of all colors and degrees. Among them we'll find images of family and friends, acquaintances and strangers and, most strangely, us, if we look truly enough into our own blinking idiocy—though that image is the last we'll recognize, so folly-free do we think ourselves to be.

We are deluded, though, as Shakespeare knows, and thus he gives us plays, for plays are dreams we enter in to see perspectively. Viewed one-way plays are artifacts, illusory spectacles we stand apart from with god-like objectivity, appraising them externally. Viewed another way they're dreams that seem but fantasies, exposing occult truths. The dreams of Shakespeare's dramas work to wake us to our slumbers, to break the dark barriers of fortified unconsciousness and let in wisdom's light. If Erasmus before him came to praise folly, Shakespeare came to bury it, but not by homily or invective, not as a preacher or a rhetor, but as a maker of mirrors by which, in Hamlet's words, he meant to show 'virtue her own feature, scorn her own image, and the very age and body of the time his form and pressure' (3.2.22–23).

Shakespeare's perplexed perspectives

When Cleopatra imagines looking at a picture of Antony, she sees in him a twofold image depending on the perspective she takes:

> Though he be painted one way like a Gorgon,
> The other way's a Mars. (ANT 2.5.116)

How (she wonders) can he be simultaneously two such opposite entities? Yet what Cleopatra sees in her lover is an emblem of what we all see in the world when we experience its duplexity; its duplicity; its twofold, oppositional, oxymoronic nature.

The world we know—life from the human perspective—seems constituted of opposing truths. Duality, bi-polarity, is its nature, sometimes manifesting itself in right/wrong, angel/devil, white/black, up/down pairs of either/or choices with positive/negative values. Then our choice seems clear if not easy. More perplexing, though, is the riper recognition that both sides of any pair we see contain positive and negative values, attractors and repulsors. Rather than the simple binary duality, we confront the complementarity of interweaving pairs such as Taoism configures in its yin/yang symbol (☯) and teaches us is the nature of the universe and us, macrocosm and microcosm.

By this conception, each of us is compounded of yin forces and yang forces, just as our bifurcated bodies stand upon two legs on which we stride alternately and on which our body either totters or balances. A good life is a difficult balancing act of learning to equilibrate between both contending goods and contending evils, and learning to cleave to some middle way between the extremes of mighty and beguiling opposites, each one a Mars and Venus, and each a Scylla and Charybdis. Such is the complex Way Things Are, and *Antony and Cleopatra* is Shakespeare's poetically dramatized *De Rerum Natura*.

What did Shakespeare believe?

My thesis about Shakespeare and religious wisdom is that, as with so many other perspectives you might assume in regarding his plays: depending on where you're standing and your angle of vision, you will see whatever you are looking for. In that respect, Shakespeare's work is like the world itself. Not only is all the world a stage, but all his dramatic stages are worlds that each of us occupies in his or her own way.

Specifically, if you are Catholic you will detect Catholicism in his plays. Likewise Calvinism, Anglicanism, paganism, animism, spiritualism, agnosticism, or atheism. If you are a student of occult Gnosticism or Kabbalahism or ancient Egyptian mystery schools or Rosecrucianism, Shakespeare will also provide you with evidence of his having been there and done that. As my own acquaintance with Taoism has grown, for instance, I've spied the Taoist sage in the Bard; in fact, I've written but not yet published an essay called 'The Tao of *Hamlet*'.

Therefore, if any writer has claim to be called 'universal', Shakespeare is a top nominee and partly for this reason: that his representation of human character, human nature, and human circumstance in the universe accords itself with all of our brave efforts to comprehend the Way Things Are. Like the universe itself, Shakespeare's plays present us with a spacious mirror. They 'hold as 'twere a mirror up to nature' (HAM 3.2.22) and we, being part of nature, see ourselves both reflected and projected. We see the universe we think we see. We see ourselves as we think we are. Shakespeare gives us ample scope to find in his representations the validation of any worldview we bring to him. Just as does the world. This argues then for Shakespeare's Cosmic Consciousness, his mystical intuition of the way of the universe, an apprehension that transcends or underlies any particular religious or secular perspective and may be called Divine.

Treachery in Shakespeare

Though I can make a good case that Shakespeare—the author of 37 plays, two narrative poems and 154 sonnets—is renowned today because of his uncanny sagacity and his metaphysical insight into the human condition, reflecting the perennial philosophy of seers and sages, I can also argue that he was fascinated with the lowest of human behavior as well as the most ethereal.

The lowest of human behavior, as exemplified archetypally by Adam and Eve (and Lucifer before them) is treachery: breaking the bond of loyal obedience. The opposite of treachery is fidelity. Thus a traitor is an infidel, a faithless forsaker of the natural bond of love, trust and kindness binding all men as brothers, all humankind as kin, for so we suppose ourselves created at our beginnings: bound blissfully in amity and concord. Thence comes Eden, our mythic image of a primordial paradise, a state of perfect love in which our species was created but which we then betrayed. In Dante's Hell, the lowest ring confines the traitors, Judas most notoriously.

Shakespeare seems, if his sonnets may be read autobiographically, to have had, early in life, a nasty experience of treachery involving a triangular sexual relationship among the Dark Lady, the young man, and himself (not to mention Shakespeare's own infidelity to his wife in Stratford). In this imbroglio he has supped full of envy, jealousy, anger, bitterness, self-recrimination and remorse. Enough, I would say, to feed an animus in every play he wrote, a festering spirit of betrayal infecting and embittering at least one character if not legions of them—so much so that I am tempted to designate treachery as Shakespeare's master theme or most obsessive preoccupation.

'Treachery! Seek it out' (HAM 5.2.312)

Traitors, treason, betrayal, treachery—what motif or motive cuts more trenchantly through all of Shakespeare?

Start with the great four. In *Hamlet* a brother betrays his brother, the king, by adultery and fratricide. In *King Lear* two daughters betray their father, who has himself, through proud obtuseness, betrayed another daughter; and then there's the dastardly bastard Edmund. Iago, feeling himself betrayed, seeks vengeful treachery upon Othello, Cassio, and Desdemona. And most blatantly, most like to Lucifer's rebellion against the Most High, Macbeth betrays the gracious Duncan, his kind king and kinsman. Even in ostensible comedies, treachery abounds. Angelo betrays Isabella, Proteus ignobly betrays Valentine. Duke Frederick ousts Duke Senior, his brother. And Helena betrays her bosom friend Hermia, who betrays her father in running off with Lysander (as does Juliet with Romeo).

While these flagrant examples spring immediately to mind, lesser treacheries can be teased from almost every work of Shakespeare's, beginning with the sonnets, presumably his most personal poetry. If their speaker is Shakespeare, the married man and father from Stratford who dallies with that Dark Lady in London, who in turn turns to the admirable young man adored by Shakespeare, then we find treachery lodged in his own heart and life. 'Treachery! Seek it out,' shouts Hamlet at the last, only to be told by the conniving Laertes: 'It is here, Hamlet, thou art slain'.

Treachery is here, everywhere, in Shakespeare's mind. His brain beats on it constantly, as does Prospero's during his twelve years of exile, preparing for improbable revenge. To wonder *why* is futile, but to notice *that* is fruitful, since Shakespeare's obsession or experience must resonate with ours. This issue of defiled loyalty and honesty must sit in the middle of our souls, an archetypal problem none can avoid and that Shakespeare had the dark insight to found his works upon.

First Lucifer turned apostate against God, then Eve and Adam followed suit, turncoats and promise breakers, reneging on the faith they had professed and sworn to keep. And so it is for all of us, we must conclude, or Shakespeare lies. His wisdom is to know our secret hearts, even though we don't confess that Thing of Darkness that possesses us: the tendency to turn and turn again against what love and loyalty bid us do.

Shakespeare's medium and message

While folly, often treacherous folly, is the stuff of Shakespeare's plays—the human medium he worked overtly in—wisdom is the message implicit in his plays, discernible to those with ears to hear and eyes to see. In the spacious mirrors of his drama, we find ourselves reflected, if somewhat distorted by the crazed and darkened glass of artful representation. Errant and bewildered, arrogant and hardhearted, vain and vicious, these simulacra of ourselves strut and fret their hour upon his stage as we do in our stage-play world, to the merriment and anguish of the angels gazing on us from their galleries above.

Yet if what we view mostly is our folly made plain, we see it now at one remove, which sets us at some distance from ourselves and opens a small gap where wisdom may peek through: 'No, I'll not be like Malvolio in his vanity, nor Iago in his envy, nor King Lear in his rashness, nor Lady Macbeth in her ambition'. In such characters we can apprehend our own tendencies toward error and correct our course. Conversely, characters like Cordelia and Rosalind, Kent and Enobarbus walk the way of loyalty and love, toward which we may reorient ourselves, ennobled by their examples. And such nobility is wisdom.

I'll leave you with one final thought to ponder regarding treachery, and a poem to sum things up. My thought is this: that the gravest treachery of all is self-betrayal, being unfaithful to what one truly is and might become, were one's essential Self to be realized in full. 'To thine own self be true' is one of Shakespeare's most famous sentences (ironically voiced by the treacherous Polonius in *Hamlet*). Arguably (though others argue otherwise), Prince Hal is such a personage, true to his highest calling of redeeming England's purloined crown.

I offer here a sonnet of sorts reflecting on both treachery and its cure.

BETRAYAL

Betrayal is the broken bond of love,
The primal eldest sin, the one above
All others in the ranks of wretchedness,
The hardest to confess and to redress,

For nothing's more essential than this bond
Of kindly kinship to which we all respond
By native impulse and by natural law:
Betraying which is mankind's gravest flaw.

Once sundered, how may it be remedied,
Remembered as the bond of all our breed,
Reknit, renewed by love's redeeming soul,
Restored to health, remade a seamless whole?

How else but by contrition, penance, prayer
Can grief allow and love begin repair?

Perennial Shakespeare

My perennial question about Shakespeare, as I have studied and taught his works for over 30 years, is to determine if his four centuries of acclaim and eminence are due essentially to his *wisdom*, a wisdom proceeding from deep spiritual insight into human nature and consciousness comparable to that of the world's great sages and seers. His plays often represent the cosmos metaphysically and depict divine and demonic presences impinging on the secular world. His imagination, at least, if not his intuition, reports on forces and entities residing in the visionary reaches beyond material mortality: spirits, specters, and deities.

More importantly, Shakespeare represents the struggle of human beings to be wise, to transcend their innate and nearly all-consuming proclivity to folly and to attain rare spiritual insight into the principles that make for ultimate human happiness, those principles revealed by our race's most enlightened luminaries. If Shakespeare's transcendental wisdom is to be truly assessed, it should not be by the acuity of his representations of metaphysical realities, but by his insight into the nature of the human heart and soul as it copes with the conditions of mortal life and either soars or sinks before it dies. Of sinking, he knew much and offered innumerable instances, but of soaring he could also report, as in his undying representations of exquisite love, of compassionate tenderness and sympathy, of joy, of courage, of fidelity, of honor, of forgiveness and redemption. He showed the best of our kind—our spiritual luminousness against the dark backdrop of our dismal follies and fallings from grace.

Though he dallied with deities and demons, Shakespeare was finally more interested in human truths rather than cosmic truths, in wisdom rather than gnosis. Whatever mythologies proved affecting for showing us our follies and pointing the way to wisdom served his turn as a dramatist whose ultimate intent was not to confirm or deny one cosmology or another, but merely to anatomize our human mortality as beings granted an opportunity that we typically fail through our foolishness to seize, wisdom being rare.

With regard to the ultimate cosmological questions we human beings ponder, questions extending beyond the bourne of natural science and into the realm of supernatural and metaphysical curiosity, what did Shakespeare believe? Specifically with respect to religious issues, what do we know or what can we infer about his credo, if he had one?

Shakespeare lived and wrote when England enforced the creed of Anglo-Catholicism upon its citizenry, though many crypto-Roman Catholics (possibly Shakespeare's own father) smoldered more or less silently in their apostasy. Even more secretly, atheists like Christopher Marlowe lived amongst the orthodox populace, while Jews, Mohammedans, wiccans, and other exotic pagans and heathens huddled beyond the pale of official credibility. Thus the credological spectrum available for Shakespeare to contemplate stretched wide and could even include the Greek and Roman pantheon; classical philosophies of stoicism, hedonism, pythagorianism, and pyrrhonism; neoplatonic hermeticism; and the homegrown lore of fairy land.

So, what did Shakespeare believe? Though most observers are naturally inclined to project their own attitudes upon an enigmatic other they cannot decipher, spying out familiar confirmations of what they already assume, Shakespeare eludes easy cosmological classification, chiefly because he never writes to us directly and expositively (as did, for instance, Sir Francis Bacon in his essays), but only through the mediation of fiction, through drama and poetry. Even his sonnets cannot be trusted to reveal his heart, nor do they clearly address the ultimate questions. In his plays, of course, Shakespeare never appears; only multitudes of characters appear, representing a plethora of attitudes and speculations about the secret workings of the universe.

No play demonstrates a variety of beliefs wider than Shakespeare's most searching and bewildered tragedy, *King Lear*. It is also his most credologically inclusive, finally leaving us in the midst of the cosmic mystery (as on a darkling plain or blasted heath) baffled in our quest for certain knowledge about ultimate issues. What Shakespeare does divulge, however, in this grim play and in other tragedies such as *Hamlet, Othello* and *Macbeth*, are human truths, existential truths, not cosmic or essential truths. Principally, Shakespeare demonstrates the primacy of love, kindness, and generosity over the fallacy of egotistical machination and monstrous malice. He reveals absolutely the dignity of selfless compassion and the wretchedness of sin. Though sinners often defeat the virtuous and sometimes go unpunished, and while even the saintly can suffer horribly, Shakespeare leaves us clear about what evil is and how it works, and likewise about goodness. We can go to Shakespeare for moral, if not cosmological, values and convictions.

What we most would like to know about our status in the universe is whether we are in good hands. We want to believe we are and that all 'evil' is either illusory or will pass at last into a greater goodness beyond our present comprehension. *King Lear* presents ambivalent responses to this query as different characters speculate variously about it. Edgar appeals to the 'kind' gods and the 'clear' gods, whereas the blinded Gloucester finds the gods malignant. Is Fortune random or predictable or controllable by will? Kent and Edmund differ in their suppositions about fate. Or is the universe simply capricious, as loony as Lear's fool appears to be, or, more aptly, as King Lear himself is in his senile imbecility?

I have a friend who is a free-thinker, a rationalist, a secular humanist, as I myself have been, though now I think of myself as a recovering secular humanist, one drawn to believe that there exist mystical insights and truths beyond the borders of my friend's skeptical scientism. Accordingly, by proper Freudian protocol, as I look about me, I tend to recognize confirmations of my own assumptions. In particular, I am naturally inclined to find Shakespeare mirroring my very point of view, just as he seems to do for all his myriad-minded readers who come away from his works reinforced in their personal beliefs, however contradictory they are to those of others. Shakespeare presents a spacious mirror, perhaps a funhouse mirror, in which we see ourselves reflected, as in a Rorschach inkblot or, more generally, in the world at large, which each of us construes idiosyncratically. So I will tell you of the worldview I discover in Shakespeare's *King Lear*, one I naturally believe is Shakespeare's own worldview objectively represented in this, his most exalted and dreadful of tragedies.

It would be easy, I think, for my skeptical friend to claim that the playwright who made *King Lear* is every inch a skeptic. One can point to the sundry assumptions of several characters who posit deities of different kinds—kind gods and malicious ones, random and indifferent gods, fiends and angels. Chiefly, one can point to the uncertainty and confusion of these characters about their own assumptions, expressing their own skepticism to undermine their beliefs. And what kind of world is it the play presents to us at the last? Not one that seems to be held in good hands, providentially cared for and redeemed from evil, loss, and sorrow; rather, a world that Kent describes as 'cheerless, dark and deadly' (5.3.291), a dreadful and despairing world of rampant injustice and malicious misery (the world, you might ruefully say, of our evening news).

Yet one could reasonably object that Shakespeare, a celebrated playwright in a theocratic state whose monarchs headed an Anglo-Catholic Government under the ultimate authority of the Christian God—that Shakespeare merely portrayed in *King Lear* the desolate state of England's pre-Christian era still benighted and unredeemed from graceless paganism. From this viewpoint, the wantonly sacrificed Cordelia foreshadows Christ crucified and portends the advent of a reformed world purged of the waywardness and wickedness represented in Lear, Gloucester, Goneril, Regan, Cornwall and, most monstrously, in the bastard Edmund. Cordelia is both wise as a serpent and gentle as a dove, as Jesus advised. While she has sharp eyes to spy out the treacherous hypocrisy of her sisters, and staunchly refuses to compromise her integrity for her own self-interest, she remains a paragon of patience, compassion, and forgiveness in her responses to her father's senile egotism and extravagant folly. One could conclude then that though *King Lear* presents us with a corrupt and fallen world vacant of intervening deities (no ghosts, no spirits, no fairies, no actual gods or demons of any sort), that in Cordelia, Kent, Edgar and the Fool he at least suggests godlike virtues that some human beings can embody even in a god-forsaken, tragic world.

Humanists can applaud this perspective and affirm as fact that human decency, loyalty, and love can contend with and sometimes prevail against human monstrosity. At our best we are able to summon selfless kindness and solicitude in the service of the humane principles of decency and justice. Even without the backing of divine exhortation and encouragement, we can find it in our own human potentiality to grow loving and wise, to transcend the wayward foolishness of our pathology and immaturity. We have it in us to grow toward godhood, an ideal we have represented in our various myths as deities whom eventually we hope to manifest in our imperfect selves.

The heart of Shakespeare

Someday I may compile a book of my essays on Shakespeare, attempting to reveal the core causes of his universal appeal and enduring esteem. I'd like to call my book *The heart of Shakespeare*, audacious though that sounds, and remembering Hamlet's warning to Rosencrantz and Guildenstern that they can never 'pluck out the heart of my mystery' (3.2.366). But the more I read Shakespeare, the less mysterious seems the business he was about as a dramatist, which has to do with anatomizing the human heart.

I use the heart metaphor in my title because what Shakespeare meant by the heart was more than the pulsing blood pump we think it to be, but rather an organ of insight and compassion that houses the essential spark of divinity in human beings. Figuratively speaking, all of Shakespeare's plays examine and diagnose varieties of cardiac problems in their principal characters: hearts that are given away, lost, assaulted, constricted, hardened, frozen, burned, and broken; hearts that need to open, soften, melt, love, and heal. 'Is there any cause in nature that make these hard hearts?' (3.6.78) laments King Lear, who suffers from his own stony heart, self-hardened apparently. Whence come cruelty, evil, and vice into human hearts, corrupting and corroding them is the issue Shakespeare investigates and reveals in play after play, the heart of our miseries. Hard hearts and soft heads are his chief concerns, our vices and our follies, and what remedies may be found for them, but mostly for our sick hearts.

The worst of all diseases in our hearts comes from betrayal. The healthy heart is a loving, giving, generous, open heart, a heart seeking connections with kindred, kindly, compassionate hearts in others through bonds of love and friendship. Hearts yearn to join amiably with other hearts and cannot live alone, lest they grow desolate and dark. Yet when a love-bonded heart is scorned and rejected by a beloved companion, great grief ensues and often great corruption. So it is with Iago, who once doted on Othello only to be supplanted by Cassio and Desdemona. Likewise is the bond of fealty between Macbeth and King Duncan cracked when Duncan promotes his boyish prince instead of valorous Macbeth as his successor. As to the heart of Hamlet, it is shattered by his father's death and by the obscene betrayal of his mother's affections for both his father and himself in her coupling with Claudius.

Sick at heart as well are other notable tragic figures in Shakespeare's cosmos: Julius Caesar ('the unkindest cut of all'), Coriolanus (betrayed by his city), Antony (a traitor to his marriage and then betrayed, he believes, by his queenly concubine), Timon of Athens (spurned by the ungrateful Athenians and driven to despair). And then King Lear ('How sharper than a serpent's tooth it is / To have a thankless child'). *King Lear* is the tale of an old man, a king, seeking to be loved yet unable to recognize love, which is invisible and ineffable, when he cannot see it or hear it. Thus, allegorically, *King Lear* is a story of the spiritual blindness of someone who seeks God but will accept only material evidence for proof of God's existence; whereas God cannot be known empirically or rationally, but only by the intuition of the heart and the insight of the soul. Just as, quite literally, Lear's friend the Earl of Gloucester cannot see the difference between the true love of his son Edgar and the feigned love of his bastard Edmund until his eyes have been destroyed; likewise, Lear is duped by the hollow protestations of love reverberating from Goneril and Regan, and he fails to appreciate the rich resonance of Cordelia's silence, which says (to those with ears to hear) that her love is immeasurable, unquantifiable, and hence unanswerable to Lear's reckoning question of *how much*.

The God of Shakespeare's Christian Bible was Love, Compassion, and Sacrifice personi-
fied, yet one who was reviled and slain by the ignorant and malignant powers of the world.
In the pre-Christian world of *King Lear*, Cordelia prefigures such a deity in her absolute
devotion, understanding, and forgiveness. Although Shakespeare presents us in *King Lear*
with a pagan and skeptical society, confused and desperate in its inability to know true love,
his own perspective transcends the dreary darkness of storm-lashed Albion and hints,
through the faithfulness of Cordelia and the loyalty of Kent, at something trustworthy and
loving at the core of the universe, a loving and merciful heart enveloped in mystery.

Heartsight: it's all about believing

> ... 'Goodbye,' said the fox. 'And now here is my secret, a very simple secret: It is only with
> the heart that one can see rightly; what is essential is invisible to the eye.' (de Saint Exupéry,
> 1943, p. 87)

It's all about believing. We are *Homo credens*, and we live by our beliefs, not by bread or by
reason alone. Shakespeare knew this about us, for make-believe was his medium. His business was making people believe, by the magic spell of his art, in the truth of his dramatic
illusions. He knew and said that 'the truest poetry is the most feigning' (AYL 5.3.20). And
though we may know few of Shakespeare's own beliefs, we may infer that he verily
believed in the powerful effect of belief itself in people's lives.

He knew how credulous we are, so easily deluded and deceived, fools of our abused
senses and aberrant fancies. Not surprisingly, many of his major characters reflect
Shakespeare's mage-like nature in their inclination to manipulate the beliefs of others:
Prince Hal, Rosalind, and Prospero for the good; Richard III, Lady Macbeth, and Edmund
for wicked ends; Oberon and Puck merely for sport.

But no character is more virtuosic in practicing the arts of reshaping others' beliefs, of
transmuting black to white and white to black than Iago, Othello's nemesis. There's not a
character in the play who is not duped by Iago's duplicity: Roderigo, Brabantio, Cassio,
Desdemona, even Emilia his wife, and all the others who call him 'honest, honest Iago'—
the cunningest, most self-conscious villain of them all, enviously diabolical to the core.

It's all about believing. Because we rarely know the truth of things, we act instead on
suppositions, on what we take for real and right, assume as true. Though the skeptical
take care to verify what they suppose is so, science is not so sure or usable as we could
wish, and much uncertainty prevails. At which point we fall back on belief. We trust and
hope it's true.

Yet one does not believe just to be a believer; one believes in order to know. Believing
is a way of knowing, a way of coming to the truth; otherwise it is nothing but simply wish-
ful fantasy and idle hope. One takes a leap of faith in the expectation of landing on firm
ground (as does Indiana Jones, quite graphically, in his search for the Holy Grail). The
presumed truth of God's beneficent and loving existence, of an almighty creative force for
good at work in the universe is not the kind of truth that science can determine through
observation, experiment, and methodological verification.

The truth of God's being, say believers, comes only by belief: believe then see; project
love and trust, reverence and wonder if you wish to find all those virtues coming back to

you, and that will be God, in truth—a universe corresponding to your belief in its goodness. God is a subjective truth, a personal truth, not an objective, public truth. God is a truth made manifest to insight, not to eyesight, seen not by the head but by the heart, by heartsight.

> 'What is essential is invisible to the eye,' the little prince repeated, so that he would be sure to remember. (de Saint Exupéry, 1943, p. 87)

Notes

1. All quotations of Shakespeare are cited from G. Blakemore Evans (1997).

Notes on contributor

Alan Nordstrom is Professor of English at Rollins College, in Winter Park, Florida, USA. He holds academic degrees from Yale University (A.B.) and The University of Michigan (M.A., Ph.D). He teaches literary and language studies, and he writes critical and personal essays and metrical poetry. His books include *The Good Life*, *According to Me*; *Living the Questions*; *Soul Search Sonnets*; and *Couplet Sonnets*.

References

de Saint Exupéry, A. (1943) *The little Prince* (K. Woods, Trans.) (New York, Harcourt, Brace & World, Inc.).

Evans, G. Blakemore (Ed.) (1997) *The riverside Shakespeare* (2nd edn) (Boston, Houghton Mifflin Company).

Jalal al-Din Rumi, M. (1995) *The essential Rumi* (Coleman Barks, Trans.) (San Francisco, HarperSanFrancisco).

Maxwell, N. (2004) *Is science neurotic?* (London, Imperial College Press).

Coda: towards the university of wisdom

Ronald Barnett

If the idea of wisdom is to do any real work for us in modern society, then the university is intimately bound up in such a project. That much has surely emerged, if only indirectly, in the contributions to this volume. It is not just that universities, collectively as a sector, have become a major set of institutions embedded within the social, economic, political and personal spheres. It is that, as sites of knowing and learning, universities are intimately connected to wisdom: there are conceptual links here. It might be objected that that observation would hold for any kind of institution concerned with knowledge and learning; or even with 'inquiry' understood more loosely; not only educational institutions but schools, museums and even newspapers could be said to come into this conceptual network – of knowledge, learning, inquiry and wisdom. But universities, surely, are particularly implicated here.

Universities are particularly implicated because of yet further conceptual connections between themselves and wisdom. For wisdom surely betokens coming at matters through broad perspectives and through a certain distancing: the wise insight is formed by bringing to bear frames of understanding altogether different from those conventionally at hand. This cognitive perspective (to use a term of Richard Peters) in turn calls for a degree of separation of the knower from the situation and for an open-endedness as to the frames of understanding that might be brought to bear. Under both of these considerations – what we might term 'epistemological distancing' and 'epistemological openness' – the university is particularly implicated. Across the world, universities prize their autonomies in part precisely because those autonomies are necessary conditions both of the university gaining a measure of separation from the frameworks of the day and of the university having access to the widest array of perspectives.

In short, if wisdom is to be regained as a project in modern society, universities bear a heavy responsibility in the matter. Universities, it may be said, live in the realm of the infinite. It is almost a *sine qua non* of the legitimate holding of the title – 'university' – that its members keep themselves open to all manner of potential frames of understanding. *A priori*, no frame of understanding can be repudiated, unless it itself comes with bigotry or closure in its wake. The forms of life that characteristically accompany the university have to be epistemologically generous or we are not in the presence of a genuine university. Universities live, too, in the realm of the complex: it is understood in its life forms that, in regard to any situation, there are multiple legitimate ways of coming at the matter and that some of these may be incommensurable with each other. The handling of dispute, conflict and complexity are all characteristic of the university; and all such capacities are necessary for the exercise of wisdom.

Universities have within themselves, therefore, many if not all of the capacities for assisting the growth of wisdom in society. The idea of the 'University of Wisdom' legitimately begins to form. Such a university would take wisdom seriously as a project, and for that, as we have just noted, a number of criteria would have to be met. This university would work, at least to a significant degree, (as Maxwell puts it) 'to achieve what is of value in life'. In realizing this aim, such a university would surely encourage broad perspectives, it would energize interdisciplinary approaches in its activities, and it would engage with society (but retain some epistemological distance from it). The process of engaging with society is crucial here since the formulation of wisdom in particular settings requires dialogue, not least in communicating and developing ideas and problem solutions.

However, the 'University of Wisdom' cannot only be outward looking. Since the notion of 'what is of value in life' is contestable, the 'University of Wisdom' would also itself constitute a space in which critical examination of that very idea would be sustained. Critical dialogue between and across the disciplines internally is a *sine qua non* of the university of wisdom achieving its potential. In turn, for that objective, leadership and even managerial effort has to be given to advancing conversation internally within the academy. The 'University of Wisdom' is characterized by weak boundaries between its academic disciplines. If the 'University of Wisdom' is, as again Maxwell puts it, 'to try to help solve…problems of living, problems of action', and then it has also crucially to attend to problems of living and of action within itself. The 'University of Wisdom' goes on developing an inward wisdom. The 'University of Wisdom' becomes wise even about itself. And herein opens a further set of issues and challenges that we can only leave hanging here.

Index

Printed in Great Britain
by Amazon.co.uk, Ltd.,
Marston Gate.